When There's a Will There's a Way

Refocusing child care practice: a guide for team managers

Sheryl Burton,
Child and Family Support and Protection Unit

The National Children's Bureau was established as a registered charity in 1963. Our purpose is to identify and to promote the interests of all children and young people and to improve their status in a diverse society.

We work closely with professionals and policy makers to improve the lives of all children but especially those affected by family instability, young children, children with special needs or disabilities and those suffering the effects of poverty and deprivation.

We collect and disseminate information about children and promote good practice in children's services through research, policy and practice development, publications, seminars, training and an extensive library and information service.

The Bureau works in partnership with Children in Wales and Children in Scotland.

Published by National Children's Bureau Enterprises, the trading company for the National Children's Bureau, Registered Charity number 258825.
ISBN 1 900900 07 5
© National Children's Bureau, 1997
8 Wakley Street, London EC1V 7QE
Printed by Futura Ltd, London E2

Contents

List of figures	v
Foreword	vi
Preface	vii
Acknowledgements	x
1. Introduction	1
2. Setting the scene	5
3. Where to begin	9
4. Working with your team	22
5. Working in the interfaces	31
6. Implementing the vision/planning the action	38
7. Sustaining the process	40
Appendix 1: The 'Once upon a time' story	45
Appendix 2: Selection of programmes (A-D) for team days	46

Appendix 3: Quiz on legislation and research	**54**
Appendix 4: The supervision contract	**65**
Appendix 5: Frameworks for auditing, mapping and evaluation of service developments	**69**
Appendix 6: Example of a user survey	**81**
Appendix 7: Exercises for individual reflection, team days and mini-training sessions	**85**
Bibliography	**112**

List of figures

Figure 1	A caricature of a child care service/ A representation of a child care service	8
Figure 2	Example of ECOMAP	34
Figure 3	Representation of the process	42
Figure 4	Representation of the process	43
Figure 5	Ethnic origin of children admitted to care 1985-87	62
Figures 6 - 9	Illustrations on mapping social work activity	70-73

Foreword

Since the publication of *Child Protection: Messages from Research* the Department of Health and ADSS together have supported a number of initiatives to promote and inform a national debate about how to build on the strengths of our work to protect children while ensuring that the full rigours of child protection procedures are only invoked when really needed, and that other children who badly need local authority support, receive it.

The debate has been a healthy one - open, frank and informed. There are signs that it has percolated into the hearts of Social Services Departments. The challenge now is to move the debate on into considered action.

This publication, based on a project funded by the Department of Health, will be helpful to all those, particularly team managers, who are striving to improve their child care practice in this way. It will be a useful aid to local teams in working out the implications of *Messages from Research* for their own practice. We know that busy team managers will not find it easy to create the space for this hard thinking. Dipping into these exercises could provide the structure that they need.

Child Protection: Messages from Research emphasised that good supervision and expert first line management are absolutely essential. This guide provides valuable materials to help achieve this.

Elizabeth Johnson　　　　　　　　　　Chris Davies
Head of Children & Families　　　　　　Vice Chair
Department of Health　　　　　　　　　Association of Directors of Social Services - Children & Families Committee

Preface

In 1995 the National Children's Bureau established a Family Support and Child Protection Unit to provide help and guidance to local authorities and other agencies facing the challenge of refocusing child care practice.

The Unit was established in response to the changes in practice and policy, indicated by the research studies summarised in *Child Protection: Messages from Research*. The researchers concluded that,

'..the balance between services was unsatisfactory... The research studies suggest that too much of the work undertaken comes under the banner of child protection... Child protection work - frequently thought of as investigations rather than enquiries - was seen to dominate... many investigations are undertaken, many families are visited and case conferences called but... in the end, little support is offered to the family.'
(Bullock 1995, pp.54-55)

The Unit's first major project was funded by the Department of Health (DH) and called 'Improving Managers' Capacity in Family Support and Child Protection Work'. The DH funded this year long initiative in recognition of the pivotal role of first level managers in developing and changing practice.

The project worked, at varying degrees of intensity, with managers and practitioners at all levels, in 12 local authorities across England, though the main recipients of input were selected social work team managers in two London authorities.

While team leaders are pivotal, they alone cannot change practice. This requires concerted efforts at all levels, including central and local political will, vision foresight and visible support from senior officers. As important are the distribution of human resources, ensuring policies and procedures support the changes, and managers and practitioners actively trying to push improvements through.

Important factors

From this work, the following factors appeared to impact significantly on the positive development of practice:

Supports

- Reliable information about research and practice developments in an accessible form;

- Awareness raising sessions across disciplines/agencies;

- Data gathering and administration systems fit for the task;

- Open review of staff, managerial and political values and attitudes towards children in need and child protection;

- Identifying, promoting and building on existing good practice;

- Having enthusiasts, optimists, innovators, 'movers and shakers';

- Having members'/senior managers' overt and active support;

- Involving users/communities in defining need and developing services at a local level;

- Unpicking the role of relevant professionals and groups such as the police, the area child protection committees and children's strategy groups etc;

- Multi-agency ownership of children's services planning process;

- Revising social work training curricula;

- Ensuring consistency of refocusing practice with in-service training plans, budgetary structures and performance indicators;

- Persistence and consistency;

- Seeing Department of Health/Department for Education and Employment/National Health Service Executive working together.

Inhibitors

- Lack of quality of information on changing practice;

- Emphasis on intellectual debate to avoid moving into action;

- Lack of family support resources;

- Lack of strategic planning structures for children's services;

- Contra motivators, for example:
  anxiety over the credibility of support versus that of protection;
  higher professional status and pay associated with child protection;
  lack of measures and indicators for preventive/support work;
  budgets structured in favour of intervention;
  range of posts and thus career opportunities reinforce child protection work;
  thresholds for intervention vary between agencies and the gap is widening;
  developing projects rather than ensuring the mainstream work changes;
  anxiety;
  fear around managing risk;

low professional esteem;
reliance on data which favours intervention;
poor understanding of statutory responsibility;
lack of emphasis on enhancing the professional knowledge of managers;
lack of machinery and guidance for collaborative working except in child protection work.

Acknowledgements

Firstly, thanks to the Department of Health for providing the financial support for this project and to members of Department of Health staff for their professional support and advice on the guide.

I would like to extend my thanks to all the team managers and practitioners who worked with me on the project and to all the members of the project Advisory Group, for their support and constructive participation: their names are listed below.

Barbara Hearn, the Practice Development Director at the National Children's Bureau and my extremely supportive and enabling manager deserves my warmest thanks. Her foresight, energy and enthusiasm have been invaluable.

Of the Bureau staff who helped on the project my special thanks go to Rachel Broad, Juleigh Gordon and Steve Howell. I thank for their calm approach, not to mention knowledge and skills. Finally a very special thanks to Marie Burton for her unfailing and unconditional support.

Sheryl Burton
Principal Development Officer
Family Support and Child Protection Unit

Members of project Advisory Group

Deborah Cameron
Ruth Gardner
Jenny Gray
Barbara Hearn
Tricia Kearney
Brian Lawson
Irene Levine

Tony Morrison
Nigel Parton
Meryl Philpot
David Shemmings
Cally Ward
John Wheeler
Sara Noakes

1. Introduction

Purpose of the guide

This 'guide' provides first-level managers at the cutting edge of refocusing child care practice, with some tips, hints and options to help them in this most complex endeavour. It is not a step-by-step manual which guarantees a particular outcome. It is deliberately brief, and is focused on ideas which managers can adopt or adapt and use according to their local context and needs.

The process outlined here aims to create or support a culture and team ethos, driven by the first level manager, that is consistent with principles of partnership, support and child-centredness. It rests on a belief that team managers are pivotal in supporting and changing practice and that their style and approach to professional guidance and management will impact significantly on the performance of the team as a whole and on that of individual practitioners.

This 'guide' will be of greatest benefit to those managers who are open and willing to try new ideas, and who see the need to continually develop and change practice. It has evolved through testing and consultation with some team leaders.

The perspective adopted

Given the need for brevity and an emphasis on the practical, there is little space for exploring and analysing underpinning theories, explicitly. In fact this has been done eloquently elsewhere and a reading list is included. The perspective adopted, however, does draw on literature and research in management and on the research basis for refocusing practice. It is informed by the author's direct experience of working with team managers in the aforementioned project and work as a social worker and manager.

The approaches suggested should help managers to negotiate their way around some of the common problems encountered in managing change, for change is central to achieving refocusing. It is not a matter of wholesale change but building on what existing support activities work well and realigning the relationship between support and protection.

There are a number of 'fallacies' associated with change outlined in greater detail by Smale (1996) but they include the observations that:

i) far from ideas cascading down the organisational hierarchy, what you commonly get is a 'trickle-down effect';

and

ii)   introducing major changes in policy and procedures with a few days' training has limited value. To achieve changes in practice far more extensive staff development activities are required;

and

iii)   some new practices will require additional resources, but this is not always necessary and is sometimes a temporary need as many will replace current ways of working.

Bear these points in mind when using this guide as an aide to your own unique approach to refocusing practice.

The refocusing of practice requires that work with children at risk of significant harm is placed within the context of family support, and that children in need become the primary group for intervention. The need for this shift has come about after a decade in which practice has been dominated by a narrow focus on incidents and investigations, and governed by increasingly tight child protection procedures.

The development of practice which supports families and protects children will require the blending of new skills and knowledge, with existing good practice, together with a thorough re-evaluation of priorities and shifts in attitudes and values.

Managers will need to be adept at managing and encouraging the adoption of new ways of working; it will be a case of persistently nudging and coaxing through new ideas.

Research on practice

A recent study carried out by researchers at York University (Fisher 1995) highlighted how little research is consciously incorporated into social work training and its limited impact on practice in the field. Practitioners gave the impression that it is exceptional for team managers to be able to share research-related knowledge and theory with them.

The tranche of research relating to child protection and family support contains important messages for practice and policy. Gibbons (1995) identified a number of key elements of good social work practice. These included qualities such as building relationships based on trust and respect; early allocation and clear planning; being able to mobilise practical and specialist help at an early stage; involving parents from the outset; having a flexible approach and the confidence to confront adults who were a danger to children. They found that:

'These qualities and skills seemed more important than technical social work methods...and also more important than comprehensive assessments in the form of DH guidelines' (Gibbons, Conroy and Bell 1995, p.105).

It is vital that managers and practitioners absorb these findings, reflect upon and relate them to their own experiences and develop practice influenced by research. The profession of social work must heed the evidence from child protection research on the unintended harm by over emphasis on forensic investigation if better outcomes for children are to be realised.

Organisational context

As important as the attitudes, skills and knowledge of first level managers is the organisational context within which they work. For such managers to flourish they need to be based in organisations which provide a supportive environment. They need senior managers who show, through actions not just words, that they encourage learning, creativity and the continual development of staff.

Skills and knowledge required

Managers at all levels will need general though core skills, transferable across agencies and sectors. These include:

- the ability to understand organisational culture and leadership;
- skills in managing change;
- skills in managing resources;
- the ability to understand the capacities and needs of their staff teams and appreciate the importance of focusing on outcomes.

Most effective will be those who are able to:

- understand the structure and culture of local authority social services departments;
- understand the breadth and flexibility of legislation and associated guidance;
- understand the complexities of the political and financial processes; and
- engage with multiple stakeholders when initiating any change.

They will need to be adept at leading yet retaining a 'marginal position' in the process. Thus they will be able to observe changes as they occur, allow others to take a significant role and will be better placed to ensure that the views of a wide range of people with different objectives and concerns are taken into account.

The refocusing of practice requires that children's needs are placed at the centre of all practice and service considerations. In addition to knowledge and skills specific to child care theory, team leaders will need skills in containing anxiety, and in managing risk and accepting uncertainty given the very public and emotionally-charged nature of child protection work.

The preceding paragraphs may have seemed very daunting for the team leader about to embark on the refocusing challenge. If so, fear not.

When There's a Will There's a Way

Philosophy

Crucial to this challenge is the philosophy of building on existing strengths; of identifying those aspects of practice and systems which will support your aims and which should therefore stay the same so then being clear about what actually needs to change and why. From this analysis of strengths and skills, ways of filling the gaps and minimising weaknesses are more likely to emerge.

Appreciating and encouraging small changes will help you to create the right environment for refocusing practice.

Finally

Experience can be a double-edged sword with confidence gained from practice being outweighed by a loss of enthusiasm, flexibility and openness.

If your most frequent response to new ideas is 'yes, but...' or 'we've tried that before...' endeavour to 'cultivate the mind of a beginner' and, 'remember: In the beginner's mind there are many possibilities, in the expert's mind only a few' (Bill O'Hanlon, 'Creating Possibilities' seminar, held at Institute for Child Health, London November 1995).

2. Setting the scene

The response to highly publicised child deaths and the subsequent inquiries in the mid-1980s and the vilification of social workers and other professionals which attended such tragic events, was the development of ever tighter and prescriptive procedures and practice guidelines and a strong focus on the development of skills in the identification, investigation and monitoring of child abuse. Recent research confirms that this has led to the polarisation of family support and child protection activities. Most resources and energy are focused on the latter, with a consequent lack of policies and resources directed at promoting children's general well-being or on ameliorating the consequences of harm suffered.

The Children Act 1989 provides the legislative framework for both supporting families and protecting children. Framed positively, with a wide definition of family support, the Act held much promise for developing services to enhance children's welfare and for working in partnership with children, families and agencies towards this end.

However the implementation of the more 'pro-active' family support requirements in Part III of the Act has been slow, patchy and highly variable.

'A broadly consistent and somewhat worrying picture is emerging. In general, progress towards full implementation of Section 17 of the Children Act has been slow.... Some authorities are still finding it difficult to move from a reactive social policing role to a more pro-active partnership role with families.' (Department of Health and Welsh Office 1994, p.16)

Similar concerns were echoed by the Audit Commission in its report *Seen but not Heard*, in 1994:

'Social services departments must develop a more proactive rather than reactive approach, paying particular attention to Part III, Section 17...'
(Audit Commission 1994a, p.3)

The context in which the Children Act was implemented accounts for the overwhelming concentration on child protection aspects.

Parton (in a speech at the National Children's Bureau conference 'Making Sense of Family Support and Child Protection', June 1995) argued that while the Children Act reforms were centrally informed by earlier research, the 'essential political momentum and catalysts for change were child abuse inquiries' of the mid-1980s.

Recent research suggests that the current system is largely effective in protecting children at the severe end of the spectrum. However there is real concern that too many children, not in need of protection, are being drawn into the system. Gibbons, Conroy and Bell (1995) found that six out of seven of those referred into the child protection system were filtered out without needing to be placed on the child protection register; and that for 40 per cent of those investigated, there was neither protective action taken nor the offer of other services.

When There's a Will There's a Way

The child protection system is in danger of becoming overloaded. Some would argue that this point has already been reached. As a consequence those children in real need of protection face an increased likelihood of being missed. Provision to meet children's general welfare needs, either in terms of prevention or for overcoming the effects of harm suffered is already severely limited. Without action to redress the balance the adverse consequences for children are considerable.

The investigation/incident-led approach tends to concentrate on procedures and prescribed tasks such as writing conference reports and organising medicals. This preoccupation can make it difficult for social workers to see the child as a whole, and to remain attuned to the child's or carers feelings about the process. Some of the key messages for effective practice are:

- *sensitive and informed professional practice;*
- *an appropriate balance of power between participants;*
- *a wide perspective on child protection;*
- *effective supervision and training of social workers;*
- *services which enhance children's general quality of life.*
(Bullock 1995, p.45)

And that:

'The most important condition for success is the quality of the relationship between a child's family and the professionals responsible.' (Bullock 1995, p.45)

Procedures and guidelines are important aids to practice when used as frameworks, rather than as blueprints for action. Their usefulness depends on the extent to which they are used flexibly, to guide decisions informed by professional knowledge and judgement and to not become 'tramlines'.

When procedures become the primary focus of concern, a dangerous and false sense of security can develop. Professionals then have a tendency to invest faith in the formal processes, as if these structures and not the work done with and by families and communities, actually decrease risk. Farmer and Owen (1995) in their research observed that one of the functions served by child protection conferences was the reduction of professional anxieties:

'The initial case conference was overtly about the management of risk, but it also contributed to the management of professional anxiety. The conference itself could be regarded as a mechanism for defusing anxiety, since it spread the risks and helped to reduce uncertainty.'
(Farmer and Owen 1995, p.85)

The formality and routine of the conference with its predictable sequence of tasks could lead to a preoccupation with procedures and a feeling that going through the formality of registering children would automatically lead to appropriate interventions to reduce risk.

'At the close of a conference there was sometimes a feeling amongst professional participants that the 'unresolved child protection issues' had been resolved by the act of registration. At the same time the inter-agency protection plan, however brief and rudimentary, helped to symbolise the fact that the child's future had been made secure.'
(Farmer and Owen 1995, p.86)

The future vision of practice is one which simultaneously protects children and supports families. In this vision children must be at the centre of changes in practice and service developments. Crucial questions must be asked throughout the process of refocusing practice about the extent to which children's needs will be met; how this will be established and how to ensure that the needs and views of children and families have maximum impact on any interventions.

This requires dynamic and child-centred practice and policies which aim to sustain children within, or connected with, their families; which meet children's needs including but not limited to the need for protection and which recognise that children have the right to be involved as people with their own views and feelings (Article 12 UN Convention on the Rights of the Child). It will mean more concentrated efforts to meet the needs of young people (over tens), who traditionally are not the central concern in child protection practice which concentrates on one- to nine-year-olds.

All those concerned with children's welfare will have to work with children, families and communities together to ensure that supportive interventions are developed which integrate the principles of Part III (family support) and Part V (child protection) of the Children Act.

The following two diagrams illustrate the position we want to move FROM and TO.

Figure 1

From **A caricature of a child care service**

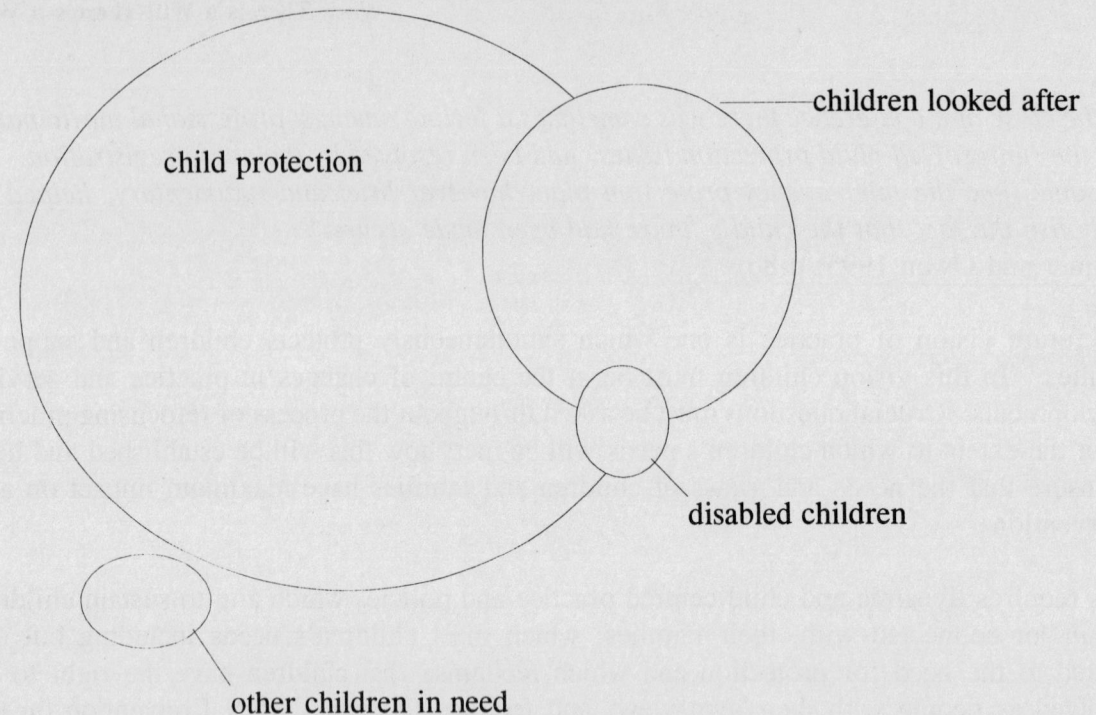

To **A representation of a child care service**

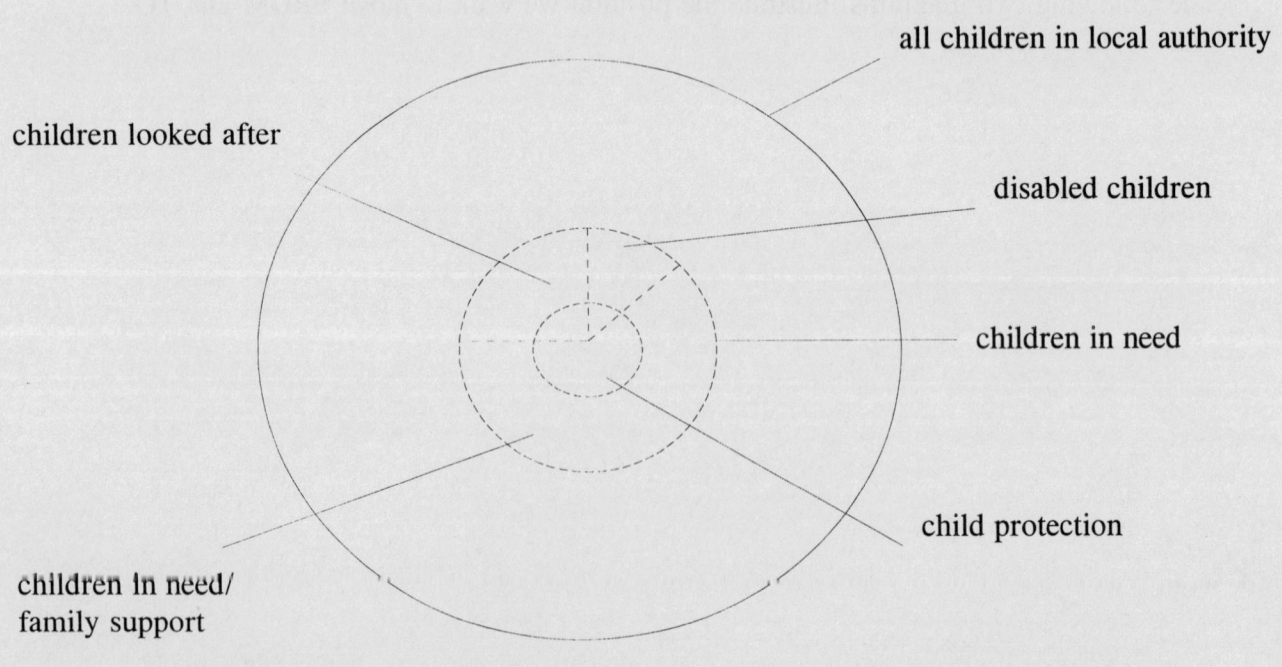

Attributed to Department of Health

3. Where to begin

Deciding where to begin is neither easy nor obvious.

Social work teams operate within a complex organisational context. Any change in practice requires attention to networks and relationships within and outside of teams/units as well as to the infrastructure.

Social work team managers participate in both management and professional systems and are the key links between the two. Team managers require knowledge of and the capacity to enable professional understanding of agency policies and priorities and of how these relate to/derive from DH guidance and policy.

Team managers are crucial to the process whereby such policies are translated into practice in a way which promotes quality services to users.

Thus, the first level manager keen to meet the challenge of refocusing practice will need to work on a number of fronts. 'Boxing and coxing', and juggling demands from above, below and sideways is a feature of team leaders' daily lives. It is a double-edged position. There-in lies the potential for influencing practice and the dangers of paralysis from excessive and contradictory demands, often combined with a lack of support and attention to their own developmental needs.

They may want to change the practice of the team they manage within the organisation, as well as the 'virtual' team, comprising themselves and other key professionals who work with children. This latter team will include, for example, teachers, police, health visitors and other professionals from both statutory and voluntary sectors.

Refocusing practice will be a journey, the beginning of which may well be marked by a mixture of anxiety and confusion, but with some hope and possibly even excitement. This guide aims to take you, the first level manager, some of the way along that journey to a position where you feel more confident about your practice, and in control of actions and developments. It provides hints, tips and signposts and some tools to help you to negotiate that journey.

You will select the route and tools appropriate to:

- where you are now;
- agency and DH policies and procedures;
- your span of control; and
- local priorities and needs.

You should anticipate returning to certain points along the route and perhaps skipping some altogether.

When There's a Will There's a Way

Thus, whilst the ideas are outlined in a sequential order, the development of practice is a dynamic process, and work will need to take place in a number of dimensions, in parallel, to get maximum benefits. Actions/events should not be one-offs and should, as far as possible be built into existing practices and systems such as supervision, team meetings, training events and even child protection case conferences.

You will have to be energetic and creative and make use of all available opportunities to raise awareness, and to get others actively assisting with promoting and progressing the change you are trying to achieve. You will have to be alert to changes in policy and practice both within and outside the agency which are likely to impact on the work. In time the work you are undertaking could itself influence the development of policy.

Self-analysis

Self-analysis is a good place to start.

Constructive self-analysis requires:

- honest and thoughtful appraisal;
- a willingness to identify strengths as well as weaknesses;
- a comparison of your self-evaluation with the views of others;
- that you set time aside for yourself or for an assessment meeting with someone else;
- that you return to some of the questions/areas over time to fill in gaps or to re-evaluate after taking steps or to address skills/knowledge gaps.

You will need to continue to reflect on and review this throughout, but it is important not to get stuck here.

Purpose of self-analysis

1. The impact of personal experience, values and attitudes on practice in social work is undoubtedly high. One of the observations made in *Child Protection: Messages from Research* (Bullock 1995) was that professionals frequently made moral judgements about families and that it was rare for proposed actions to be based on research evidence about outcomes for children. One purpose is therefore to increase awareness of your own value positions and their influence on what you see as good practice, and your expectations of the team.

2. A second purpose is to identify and be explicit about the knowledge on which practice is based.

3. Extrapolating from the above, another purpose is to identify the gaps in knowledge, skills and experiences which it may be necessary to fill in order to manage effectively the refocusing of practice.

Questions/areas to think about

1. What is your response to the pre-conditions for effective practice highlighted in *Messages from Research* (listed on p.6 of this guide)?

2. Where do you locate yourself on the 'child rescue' vs 'family preservation' continuum? Why do you place yourself there?

3. Where has most of your practice experience been acquired? Who or what has most influenced your approach? How have you learnt from your experience? Which case will you always remember? What is the message from that case?

4. Assess your knowledge base:

- What theoretical perspectives underpin your practice?
- What have you read recently?
- What do you read in full/what do you dismiss?
- What do you highlight for others to read?

Consider what all this says about your practice and approach to work with children and families and then note the gaps in your knowledge which you need to address. How does your experience and knowledge relate to a future vision of practice?

5. Do you see yourself as:

- a 'reflective' manager:

'a facilitator whose role is to help find an optimal course of action or solution to problems in an uncertain world' and who *'will use all sources of relevant knowledge'*, who thinks that *'professional development occurs through a process of experiential learning from (rather than by) doing. Learning is through analysis by observing, reflecting, experimenting and conceptualising.'* (Jones and Joss 1995, pp.26-27. See also Schon (1983 and 1987) for fuller exposition on reflective practitioners.)

or
- a practical professional, who thinks that:

'the knowledge base is practical knowledge (know-how) generated from work situations' (Jones and Joss 1995, p.23) with a mix of common sense, a theoretical approach and a view of professional development as occurring through learning 'by doing' (Jones & Joss, 1995).
or
- a professional who has technical knowledge and a value system which is problem- rather than client-centred?

When There's a Will There's a Way

6. Analyse your skills

Do your own self-evaluation using the following questionnaire then ask team members, line managers, colleagues within and outside of the agency to complete it. In fact, ask anyone you feel is in a position to give you useful feedback. The questionnaire can be photocopied. Replies can be anonymous.

Questionniare for evaluation of skills and attitudes		
Please share with me your perception on my a) skills and b) attitude to the following: Mark using the scale 0 to 10 where 0 = worst/negative and 10 = best/positive. Answer as many questions as you can.		
	Skill	Attitude

1. Assist workers to assess the needs of:
   a. the child
   b. the family
   c. the community		

2. Assist workers to assess risks to:
   a. the child
   b. the family
   c. the community		

3. Enable workers to access and develop resources		
4. Able to support measured risk taking		
5. How far does my management practice as you experience it: a. meet the values of anti-discriminatory practice? b. encourage working in partnership with children and families? c. promote interaction and development of links with local people and groups? d. encourage developing networks of support and acting through those networks to get practical outcomes for children and families? e. provide supervision to individual workers which incorporates the key elements of management; support; education and development? f. which elements of supervision are given most emphasis? Add any comments on changing supervision to support refocusing practice.		

g. how much do I consult with/feedback to and generally involve my line manager in the team's work and concerns?		
h. help those I work with to deal with anxiety and uncertainty?		
i. manage the workloads of the team and individuals?		
j. how well do I enable workers to engage in work other than individual casework and undertake activities designed for development?		
k. promote a pro-active approach to the work?		
l. meet your needs for decision-making which involves the team and significant others in the process?		
6. How much do I encourage a culture of analysing and questioning practice?		
7. Is the culture in the team one which encourages sharing of information and new ideas?		

8. How much do I, model the principles? delete as appropriate
      empowerment; a little/a lot/not at all
      partnership; a little/a lot/not at all
      openness; a little/a lot/not at all		

9. How much do I display a commitment to continually evaluating and developing practice? A little/a lot/not at all		
10. How much do I display a commitment to involving children, families and communities in the development of practice and services? A little/a lot/not at all		
11. Where would you place me, on a scale of 0 to 10 in terms of my current capacity for managing the refocusing of child care practice?		
12) Any other comments or advice?		

When There's a Will There's a Way

What was your response to the idea of getting feedback from others? What might that say about your management style? Is your approach consistent with achieving a refocusing of practice?

Look at similarities in replies between different respondents and identify themes you should address. Compare the team view and your line manager's view against your self-analysis.

You may wish now to share the outcome of this evaluation with a trusted colleague and your line manager as part of preparing your personal action plan.

Filling the gaps

A crucial aspect of the self assessment is understanding how you learn. It is important not only for your own self-knowledge, but for your team. Understanding how adults learn is vital for changing practice, and understanding yourself is a good starting point. Morrison observes that *'understanding how adults learn and being able to apply this in practice is ...fundamental to effective supervision'* (Morrison 1993, p.45).

The following recommendations are given in that context. It is for you to determine which methods are most likely to facilitate change and enhance your learning.

1. Knowledge

If there is a gap in your knowledge of recent research and reports, pertinent to the refocusing of practice, then you could address this by reading all or part of the following texts and articles:

Audit Commission, (1994) *Seen but not Heard: Co-ordinating Community Child Health and Social Services for Children in Need. Detailed Evidence and Guidelines for Managers and Practitioners.* HMSO

Bullock, R, and others (1995) *Child Protection: Messages from Research.* HMSO

Davies, C, and Little, M (1995) 'Family circle', *Community Care,* no.1073 (22 Jun) pp18-19.

Department of Health and Welsh Office (1994) *Children Act Report 1993.* HMSO

Department of Health and Welsh Office (1995) *Children Act Report 1994.* HMSO

Edwards, C.(1995) 'Are children better off following protective interventions?', *Child and Family Law Quarterly*, vol.7, no.3 (Sep) pp.136-151.

Hearn, B. (1995) *Child and Family Support and Protection: A Practical Approach.* National

Children's Bureau

NCH Action for Children (1996) *Children Still in Need: Refocusing Child Protection in the Context of Children in Need*. NCH Action for Children

Burton, S (unpublished) *Research Summaries on Child Protection and Family Support*. National Children's Bureau

These are relatively short and accessible articles and texts. If you have time to read more then try the original research studies and *'Making Enquires into Alleged Child Abuse and Neglect: Partnership with Families'* edited by Dendy Platt and David Shemmings. (Pennant Professional Books.)

In addition you should:

- Use the exercises to be found in the appendix of this guide, for example the knowledge-based quiz (Appendix 3a) and the exercise based on the Farmer and Owen (1995) findings (Appendix 7d).

- Consider whether the department has a policy on assessment? Does it fit with/support your approach? How? If not, what needs to change?

- How are assessments of children and families undertaken in practice? Is this consistent with practice leading with children in need?

- Speak to colleagues, the training department, your manager about particular experts whom it may be valuable for you to meet.

- Use supervision to monitor, challenge and develop your knowledge.

- In addition or alternatively you may be able to locate a mentor, within or outside of the organisation.

2. Skills and/or experience gap

- Find appropriate training or workplace-based opportunities for developing new skills or stimulating ideas. For example involve the team in creating a community profile of resources and needs.

- Visit places and find out about projects. For example, the Hayle project in Cornwall, or 'The Playden' in Newcastle which was the subject of of an article in *Community Care* (Mercer, C 'A winning prescription', *Community Care* 5 Oct 1995, p.24.) Family Partnership Team recently launched by Kensington & Chelsea (Linehan, T 'The family way' *Community Care*, 22 Feb 96. p.10). Contact Exploring Parenthood

When There's a Will There's a Way

for information on The Moyenda Project and its report on the support needs of black parents.

- Find other examples from recent *Community Care* articles.

- Subscribe to '*The Family Support Network Newsletter*' published by University of East Anglia and Keele University which is a useful source for new developments. Make contact with key people in these initiatives, who may have experience which helps you avoid reinventing the wheel, and in those listed in *Children Still in Need* (NCH Action for Children 1996).

- List all the fora (within and outside the department) you are currently involved in and reflect on how you use them. How could you use them differently?

Useful addresses and telephone numbers:

- Exploring Parenthood
  National Parenting & Development Centre
  4 Ivory Place, 20a Treadgold Street, London W11 4PB
  Tel: 0171-221 4471

- Family Support Network
  c/o Sue Bailey
  School of Social Work, Elizabeth Fry Building
  University of East Anglia, Norwich NR4 7TJ
  Tel: 01603-593557/593532
  Fax: 01603-593552

- Parenting Education and Support Forum
  National Children's Bureau, 8 Wakley Street, London EC1V 7QE
  Tel: 0171-843 6000
  Fax: 0171-278 9512

Where you have a skill gap, talking and meeting with others will help you map out how crucial this gap may be and how to fill it. Talking with people should not add a burden.

At the same time you and your team could be looking for opportunities to gain new skills and expand experience. For example, becoming involved with a new project or initiative such as joining the core group exploring the potential for using the Family Group Conference model; or taking a lead role in reviewing the needs of the 16+ age group; or becoming involved in the local 'keep children safe' initiative.

'We decided as a team that even though it would be hard working in Investigation and

Assessment it was important to be involved in some development work. One worker was given the space and time to research current resources for the 16+ age range who represented a high percentage of the referrals to our team but who received very little. She has reported back and has found out about all sorts of hostels and provisions that the rest of us know nothing about. She has also said that it has been really interesting and that people have been far more open to meeting with her than she ever expected'. (Team leader)

Below are case studies which illustrate the outputs of three team managers from looking at their attitudes/skills/knowledge. We will then follow one manager through the process outlined in the guide.

Case studies

Joan - team manager A

Joan has been managing a children and families team for three years. She believes strongly that managers should be involved, help out on duty, and in effect should manage 'by walking about'.

Before joining this team she had worked in an area with a very diverse population and with a high level of community activity. She had been involved in promoting such work herself, for example helping to establish a Saturday School, and working with the health visitor to set up a support group for young black lone mothers. She remembers fondly her days as a practitioner in a team with a strong focus on prevention but it feels like a long time ago and while she still believes strongly in the approaches used, she is no longer confident in her own skills.

The team she now manages, compared to others in the department has, she believes, a fairly strong preventive ethos, with comparatively low numbers of children on the child protection register and little involvement with courts, but with substantial numbers of cases that she would categorise as 'children in need'. Several members of the team are highly skilled in child protection work. Joan chairs Child Protection conferences, and has been on a Family Rights Group course for chairpersons and has taken an internal course on the supervision of child protection work.

However, the team links with, and active support of, small voluntary and community groups is far less than she would like. She wants the team to look at other approaches, and not be so stuck on individual casework. She would like practitioners to take a more active role in making links with local groups, as she is the only one sustaining any active involvement at present. Their reliance on her as a black manager to promote links with black and minority ethnic groups in the area was something she has been trying to address.

Joan likes to be in the thick of things, and does not find much time for reflecting and keeping up with theory and research. She scans articles in *Community Care* and attends internal and external training courses, when she catches sight of them.

When There's a Will There's a Way

She welcomes the opportunity that the refocusing debate has allowed her, to reflect on and analyse what, how and why she does things.

Outcome of self-analysis

Joan thinks that her experience, belief and values are compatible with achieving the refocusing of practice. Feedback from her manager and staff team, and from her fellow team leaders confirmed this. She had not asked anyone outside of the organisation for feedback. She realised through this process that her network was not as extensive nor as dense as she had thought, and that she would need to resurrect dormant networking skills.

Team members fed back that she was knowledgeable about procedures and local resources, and that exploration of practice issues and new ideas was not discouraged but only happened sporadically. However they did not find her well-informed on research and practice developments and felt that she could do more to keep up to date and could be more pro-active in her approach to practice issues.

Joan's action plan:

1. To read *Child Protection: Messages from Research* (Bullock 1995) and pull out key points for the next management meeting.

2. To raise the idea of a team day to develop a vision and action plan for future practice with regard to team development and working with local networks.

3. To contact the coordinator of the multi-disciplinary child protection forum to get refocusing practice onto the agenda.

4. To widen her range of contacts by finding a forum outside of the authority which would enhance stimulation and ideas. Joan agreed to contact National Institute for Social Work to find out more about the practice and development exchange model.

Sarah - team leader B

Sarah qualified as a social worker in 1989. Before doing the course she had acquired a degree in social administration and had spent six months as a volunteer with the probation service, followed by six months as a probation assistant.

Since qualifying she has worked in specialist children and families teams, including a two year spell with the NSPCC as a child protection officer. She came to this borough to take up her team leader post two years ago. She supervises a team of five social workers. She believes in systematic and close management and uses the department's caseload weighting system. She is keen to implement the supervision policy and the new appraisal system. Supervision is regular and focused. Everyone in her team has been through the in-house child protection training on recognition and investigation, assessment and memorandum interviewing. In the team's small library are all departmental policies and procedures relating to children; the *Children Act 1989* (HMSO, 1989) and the *Children Act 1989 Guidance and Regulations. Volume 2: Family Support, Day Care and Educational Provision for Young Children* (HMSO, 1991); *A Child in Trust: The report of the Panel of Inquiry into the Circumstances Surrounding the Death of Jasmine Beckford* (Brent Council, 1985) and *Whose child? The report of the public inquiry into the death of Tyra Henry* (Lambeth Council, 1987); and a range of texts on child abuse including Adcock, White and Hollows' *Significant Harm: its management and outcome* (Significant Publications, 1991) and David Jones' *Understanding Child Abuse* (Macmillan, 1987).

The team is seen as very efficient and are regularly commended on the quality of their court reports by the legal section. They have the highest numbers of children on the child protection register and all these cases are allocated. The unallocated list consists mainly of adolescents being looked after or at risk of entering the system. There is a high level of referrals for therapeutic work to Child Guidance, and strong links with the police, health visitors, educational pychologists and the local NSPCC family centre which works with children on the register and their families.

Outcome of self-analysis

Sarah placed herself in the middle of the rescue versus preservation continuum, after a lot of thought and uncomfortable feelings about her attitudes and assumptions. She realised that she had very little in-depth knowledge of voluntary organisations and community groups and that whilst she read a lot and encouraged her staff to do so, much of it was about child abuse.

The team made positive comments about her systematic approach and appreciated her confidence and knowledge of the literature and procedures relating to child abuse.

They did comment however, that they found her style, interventionist and that they did not feel particularly involved in decision-making; the supportive aspects of supervision needed greater attention. They said that there was little opportunity to consider approaches or work beyond cases on the Child Protection Register and children 'looked after'. They confirmed what she herself had identified as a major gap, her knowledge of and interaction with local agencies, professionals and groups apart from those with a strong child protection focus.

Sarah's action plan

Sarah would read:

Crosbie and Vickery (1989) *Community Based Schemes in Area Offices*. NISW
Department of Health (1991) *Patterns and Outcomes in Child Placement: Messages from Current Research and their Implications*. HMSO
Edwards, C (1995) 'Are children better off following protective interventions ?' *Child and*

Family Law Quarterly, vol.7. no. 3 (Sep). pp. 136-151
NCH Action for Children (1996) *Children Still in Need: Refocusing Child Protection in the Context of Children in Need.* NCH Action for Children.

Sarah would also:

- Attend a one day course at the Family Rights Group on 'Reunification, a neglected route to permanence'. Others had attended the course, and felt it gave them access to research on reunification which they had previously been unaware of.

- Do Exercise 6 from *Child Protection: Messages from Research* 'What happens in your local child protection system', over the next month (Appendix 7g of this Guide).

- Facilitate a team discussion of the main points from Carolyn Davies' and Michael Little's article 'Family circle', *Community Care* 22 Jun 1995, pp.18-19.

Gerald - team leader C

Gerald has been a team leader, in this authority for seven years, and has been qualified for 20 years. Most of his contemporaries are now either senior managers, in this or neighbouring authorities or else they had left social work.

Gerald has seen so many shifts and trends in social work he finds it hard to get worked up about it any more. He did enjoy his time as a patch-based social worker. Although he would like to believe it were possible to return to more 'preventive' work, he couldn't see it happening. Things had changed too much and what with the lack of resources and staffing problems, it all seemed like a pipe dream. Senior managers were forever restructuring, so efforts to develop practices are always overridden.

He rarely goes on training courses outside the department and although he scans *Community Care* is not one for reading too much. However, his manager did persuade him to go to a regional event, disseminating *Child Protection: Messages from Research* (Bullock 1995) and he had found it surprisingly interesting. It made him think a lot about the things he used to be good at, such as networking with other agencies and groups, and the rapport he had with the families he worked with.

Outcome of self-analysis

Gerald had very large gaps in his knowledge of research and the issues arising from them; he wasn't seen as pro-active or encouraging of questioning approaches to practice and his attitude to team ethos and to practice was a very 'common sensical' one. The general feeling was that he probably did 'have it' once but there were serious questions about his motivation and capacity to change now.

Gerald's action plan

- To present to the management team key messages from the conference he attended.

- To read the shortest articles on the reading list from the conference and circulate them for others in the team to read.

- To locate a mentor, who was not his line manager. His manager agreed with this, and they both set out to do some informal searching.

- To attend the department's supervisors' group which he had previously dismissed as a 'talkshop'. Maybe there was a way of making it more useful to him.

- To discuss with the team ways of promoting practice development. He was particularly keen on doing a skills audit, having reconnected with some of his own strengths and skills, which had lain dormant for some years. His team might similarly find some untapped potential.

Having undertaken a self-analysis and compared this with other people's perception of your skills, knowledge and attitudes, you now need to move on to working towards change with the team.

4. Working with your team

For practice to develop you will need to be working with the team as a whole, and with the individuals within your team. This will ensure that both team and individual needs for support, guidance and development are met. While in this guide, more attention is given to working with the team as a whole, individual supervision and team development should go hand-in-hand.

Supervision

Supervision informed by research and good practice is central to the development of practice and services to meet the needs of children and families. It is essential that the supervisory process receives constant care and attention.

All too often there is a common risk that the needs of the organisation can supercede the needs of workers, with management overwhelming professional concerns and development. The role of supervision in the development of professional practice must be clear and not diminished with the growth of a general management culture in social services. The need for supported professionally strong practice is borne out by inquiries and observations made in the National Children's Bureau project, 'Developing Good Practice for Staff New to Child Protection Work'.

Working to improve supervision, while developing a team ethos for sharing information and practice-based discussions, lays a good foundation for changing and improving practice.

'I found it helpful to focus on improving my supervision. I used some of the material from Tony Morrison's, 'Staff supervision in Social Care' especially the 'reflections' sections. I became more rigorous about having a contract, establishing mutual expectations and discussing possible power issues. There is also a system for reviewing if and how needs and expectations are being met. Sessions are more structured and planned and workers say that there is now more emphasis on their development and training needs'. (Team leader)
(See Appendix 4 for a format for a supervision contract, some guidance notes on reaching an agreement and a sample of Tony Morrison's 'reflections' exercises.)

Developing a team ethos for practice development

Make one of your key objectives the development of a team culture in which team discussion of practice issues becomes a regular occurrence. Use existing meetings, such as team meetings, team time, professional discussion slots, away days, area days and management meetings to best effect to focus on practice and to encourage workers to reflect and share ideas and information. Use the exercises in *Messages from Research* and *Challenges to Partnership in Child Protection Practice* and those exercises included in Appendix 7 of this

When There's a Will There's a Way

Guide. Criteria for decision-making; the implications for practice arising from *Messages from Research* and the integration of assessment of needs and risks are some topics which will engage practitioners.

Look at the way meeting time is currently used. Ask yourself and the team if it is really necessary to spend two hours on business and to routinely go through all the cases in the 'allocation basket' every week, only to leave them there at the end. There is experience of some teams which have three hour team meetings and others which deal with the business in no more than an hour and have separate practice discussions or skills-based slots. The latter is by far the more stimulating and enriching environment for developing practice.

Creating a vision with your team

You will need to agree a team away day to engage your team in looking ahead to a vision of refocused practice, and to begin to map out and take steps towards realising that vision.

Before the session you should circulate brief articles, for example those listed earlier in 'Filling the gaps'.

You should be analysing team culture and knowledge as outlined in later sections.

Start off the session by reading the story 'Once upon a time...'(Appendix 1). Facilitate a team discussion of the issues raised by this story, and in the articles circulated.
Engage the team in mapping out ways forward for developing practice.

Exercise: our way ahead

Begin by suggesting that team members project forward two to three years from now. Encourage them to be open and creative, but to retain a sense of reality. Point out that the economic and social context has not altered significantly.

Against this backdrop invite them to call out their initial thoughts, on the key elements of their 'vision of practice which supports families and protects children.' Note these on a flip-chart.

They can then work in pairs to further develop and negotiate the vision and then together as a team. They should then be able to encapsulate the team vision of practice, in no more than two paragraphs.

Initial action plan

Having created a vision, you will need to work with your team on mapping out what needs to change in order to realise that vision.

Essentially you will have to be considering:

'Who will need to do what and with whom' in order to move towards your vision.

Crucial to the process will be making sure that those things which are supportive of your vision, and therefore need to be sustained, are identified.

Together with your team you need to identify all the significant people with knowledge or expertise. You will need, for example, users and potential users, influential senior managers, other team leaders and practitioners, key people in health, education, the police, community leaders (those likely to influence views), council members and those in charge of finance. All may have to be engaged in order to progress ideas.

At this stage actual knowledge of people's views and positions on what you are trying to do will be sketchy, and you will therefore need to continually reassess this initial map. You should have a clear strategy for engaging them in the process.

Log changes occurring in the wider organisation which will support or inhibit progress, and think of ways of harnessing supports and diminishing blocks. For example, how flexible are existing policies and procedures such as the eligibility criteria for children and families to access services? What scope is there for you and the team to impact on these procedures?

If there are cost or resource implications in these changes, might it be possible to achieve these through working with another agency(ies)? While working in this way, you and the team will need to recognize and work within boundaries and systems of accountability. Simultaneously, seek to influence the development of procedures and policies which support children and families and locate child abuse within a children in need context.

Knowing there are people beyond your agency in positions of power who support your direction will help you face the many challenges that will cross your path on the journey, for example, the Department of Health and ADSS support for the dissemination of *Messages from Research*. Find out about others too.

'We have now had two team workshops on 'The Way Forward'. The team knew in advance that the title was 'Creating a Vision for Supporting Families and Protecting Children'. I gave out copies of two short articles on family support in advance. Everyone came. I was really surprised at how keen they were. They'd read the materials and had made notes. Someone even came in from annual leave'. (Team Leader)

Skills map for the vision/skills audit for the team

You have created the vision, related your vision to the organisation's mission, mapped out what needs to change, and identified the crucial players within and outside of the organisation. You should now focus on identifying the skills necessary for achieving the vision, and for future practice built on the foundation provided by consistent organisational culture, plans and policies. Match the vision against the existing skills within the team. The required skills/knowledge may be available from elsewhere within the organisation.

When There's a Will There's a Way

Work out:

The vision	Skills needed to meet the vision	Current skills within the team	Gaps	Filling the gaps How/who Within/outside org.

There should be an agreed time-scale for implementing the initial plan of action for the team. Awareness raising and information gathering and sharing will continue throughout, but without setting a deadline for the initial phase, it could become an end in itself.

The initial action plan should include measures of success. How will we know when we have got there? What will have changed? At this stage they are likely to be interim measures (see Appendix 5c for brief notes on Monitoring and Evaluation).

The above outline may read as though engaging the team in creating a vision of practice which supports families and protects children, is simple and straightforward. In reality it may be, but a lot will depend on the culture, history and existing practices, and the morale of the team and the wider organisation. It is likely to take significantly more time than a single team session to reach this point and you will have to facilitate discussions and debates about the need for and the consequences of refocusing practice but this should not be used as an excuse for no action.

Members of the team may well be in different positions. The skill is in working with these differences positively and effectively. The message should be that a range of different perspectives, knowledge and skills are needed and that not everyone has to hold exactly the same views and be equally adept in the same areas of practice. But they do need to own the vision and to see where and how they fit into the whole picture, and augment the repertoire of skills, knowledge and experiences contained within the group. For example, those who have built up a considerable amount of experience and skills in child protection investigations will be a major resource to the team and can lead in that area. Similarly team members with knowledge of welfare rights could provide a direct service to users and act as consultant and trainer to other social workers. Other members with experience of community social work could help with mapping and assessing needs.

To ensure that the team is not becoming an 'island' it may be useful at this stage to share the work of the team with key senior managers. If the culture is an open one this will be mutually beneficial. If you are working in a defensive culture then sharing your progress will help ensure acceptance and ownership. Be prepared to make adjustments if a senior manager identifies wider political consequences arising from your vision.

When There's a Will There's a Way

Analysis of team practice and culture

An analysis of the team practice and culture will help establish the degree of congruence between the changes you are trying to bring about and the team capacity and ethos. This analysis should be ongoing.

'Looking at where we are now; what we do; which agencies we work with; what networks or resources we are aware of, has helped us to get a wider view of family support'. (Team Leader)

The following are some questions you should seek to have answered. This can be achieved through collating and analysing data, observations, initiating discussions and organising specific team events. Some it will be possible to answer straight away, others will need ongoing observation and analysis.

Analyse practice

Reflect upon and discuss with your line manager/mentor/team members:

1. Are children and families central, or peripheral to the team's current approaches and systems? What evidence is there to support this view? What systems are there for gathering the views of children and families?

2. What is the balance in the team's workload in terms of casework vs groupwork vs development of links\support networks in the community?

3. What happens to referrals? Do exercise 6 from *Messages from Research* (Appendix 7g) 'what happens in your local child protection system?' Get better information about this, and see whether policy and practice developments are necessary.

4. What is the composition of the team, in terms of background, qualifications, experience and ethnicity. What is the rate of staff turnover?

5. What skills are there within the team? Are they appropriate to the range of activities and tasks needed to achieve the vision?

6. What assessment frameworks are used by the team? Do these frameworks integrate assessment of need with risks?

7. Does the department have a policy on assessment? Is the team aware of the presence/absence and the implications of such a policy?

Try the following frameworks with the team.

(i) Pauline Hardiker's grid (Appendix 5a) to map out at which level most of the team's efforts are currently targeted.

(ii) Smale and others 'Framework for Social Work Activity' map out some typical cases and see to what extent activity occurs on the right side of the map. Refocused practice would typically spread across the whole framework (Appendix 5b).

When There's a Will There's a Way

> **Analyse the team culture**
>
> 1. Does the team have a shared understanding of aims, objectives and priorities?
>
> 2. What are the team's stated values and principles?
>
> 3. How do these match with what actually goes on, for example, saying that there is a prompt response to referrals and then having a waiting list of two months; saying that the team is responsive and flexible, but opening the office for set hours each day and only offering office appointments?
>
> 4. What attitudes are there to time-keeping? Working late? Attending team meetings? Going on training courses? How consistent are these with networking, meeting community groups, developing services and so forth?
>
> 5. How are new members inducted, in both formal and informal ways? What information are they always given, and what are they left to find out?
>
> 6. Do discussions of equal opportunities issues suggest a high profile and commitment? Is this manifested in any visible ways, for example, composition of staff team; career progression of women; career progression of workers with disabilities of black and minority ethnic workers; client groups worked with; community groups linked with?
>
> 7. What is the ratio of work on individual cases and other work such as groups and projects?
>
> 8. What is the team's perception of its links with others within and outside of the organisation?
>
> 9. How does the team respond to change? Think of an occasion when you introduced a change? How did the team respond and what enabled the change to happen?
>
> 10. Where are the most influential relationships for the team, for example, team member is married to head of police child protection team; three staff trained together at Tavistock Clinic; two members were based in a patch office etc.

'Creating a team environment for sharing the research, new ideas and thinking about practice has encouraged workers to analyse their work, to become better informed themselves, and to show greater clarity and confidence in their approach to the work.

Others have observed that the team's work has noticeably improved, with more considered and well-analysed decisions. We now think about family support in all circumstances and see it as enveloping all activities rather than as something separate. I would say that this has led to much better partnerships with families and more pro-active networking with other agencies'. (Team Leader)

Team knowledge

The quiz (Appendix 3) is one you can use with the team in full or in part. Experience with team leaders suggests that it will be a useful, if painful, exercise.

It can be used as a tool for assessing knowledge gaps in the team, and deciding on what reading materials to distribute, to acquire and to bring to team meetings. Individuals could take responsibility for reading and summarising reports articles/books and doing brief presentations in team meetings.

A shortened version of the quiz can be a useful lead in to a practice discussion/workshop.

Continuing Joan's story

Joan had agreed that she would facilitate a team day, with the focus on creating a vision for future practice. A month passed during which she was able to prepare for the day while continuing her usual daily work.

During this time Joan read *Child Protection: Messages from Research* (Bullock 1995), and circulated two key articles from *Community Care* supplements, one by Michael Little and Kathleen Taylor, 'Balance of power', *Inside Community Care*, 27 July 1995, pp.2-3 and another by Owen Gill, 'Neighbourhood watch', *Community Care*, 8 Jun 1995, pp.30-31

The team day began with a lively debate about the issues raised. Several team members found the research conclusions confirmed of their current practice, others felt they were being attacked for doing their level best to protect children, and all were anxious that if changes were introduced they had to be supported by policies and procedures.

The second hour was spent creating a vision that they were all able to sign up to. Joan prompted and challenged, continually seeking to bring the team back to the needs and perspectives of children, their families and local communities.

They agreed that developing 'collaborative working practices' was to be a central theme in their vision. They wanted to improve on 'working in partnership' in all aspects of their work with children, with families and with communities and with other agencies, such as schools. Joan's analysis of referrals had revealed a number of children aged nine to ten years on the verge of being excluded from school whose parents were 'at the end of their tether', and

When There's a Will There's a Way

were requesting 'care'.

They began to map out what needed to change and what should stay the same in order to achieve these goals.

Through creating the skills map for the vision, and auditing team skills they found out that one team member had, in the past, been a primary school teacher and had acquired considerable skills in networking with education professionals and in engaging parents in activities. This was helpful when devising strategies for engaging schools and parents to find ways of working to support children at risk of exclusion.

Important gaps included a lack of recent experience of consulting with children and families about needs and how these were being met by the services currently available.

The session as a whole was very stimulating. The team not only learnt enormous amounts about each other's perspectives and skills, but also found out about key policy developments and people within and outside of the organisation. They found themselves wondering:

- Which other teams and managers were doing this?

- What was happening about the children in need policy?

- How appropriate were the performance indicators?

- Were the child protection procedures going to be changed?

- What was happening about awareness raising in other agencies?

Asking these questions opened up channels of information they had previously been unaware of.

5. Working in the interfaces

A social services children and families team interfaces with a range of groups and individuals, any or all of whom could have an impact on achieving the future vision of practice. All these groups have to be engaged with and enabled to 'buy into' the changes that the team is promoting as each has a stake in the way that the team practices. Changes have to be congruent with organisational policies and require the support/permission of those responsible for policy development.

The key interfaces are:

- child(ren);
- family(ies);
- community;
- rest of own organisation;
- other organisations.

'Grasping opportunities' could become the team 'buzz phrase' for 'working the interfaces'. Given the climate of high demands and limited resources and time, you will need to make the most of existing mechanisms and fora to raise awareness and stimulate ideas.

Inter-agency interface

- Raise the debate at inter-agency fora such as child protection conferences, inter-agency workshops, reviews of looked after children, needs assessment conferences, crime prevention strategy groups, child safety groups, professionals networks.

- Put it on the agenda in advance and consider circulating summaries of the current debate in advance, and the team vision.

- Make sure that those who are responsible for organisational policies and procedures are fully informed and consulted.

- Make sure that people feel that their views on the team's future direction are important.

- Give them the opportunity to comment in a structured way, for example asking for their anxieties, fears and hopes, their ideas and suggestions. Control the time allowed for this and tell them how the team will feed back future plans and actions, and how their views have been incorporated.

- Record what people say. Accept that they may express more about their concerns and anxieties than putting forward ideas which will direct you on how to focus work. **The crucial issue at this point is to keep people involved and to cultivate allies, not create enemies.**

- Go back to your map of key people to involve and see if there are gaps in relationships, which may require special meetings in order to share the team's ideas and the process with new partners.

- Aim to get key people to actively support the team's vision. They are more likely to do this if they have seen they can influence it. Beware of vested interests and getting caught in power disputes. However, you are already on the right track, and involving them in discussions from the start is one way of ensuring support.

Interfacing with the rest of your organisation

The organisational context - the structure, culture and administrative arrangements - can be very influenctial in the development of practice.

It is therefore essential that managers/teams carry out an analysis of the people, policies and other factors likely to support or inhibit changes in practice.

Being part of an organisation that encourages departments/managers and teams/practitioners to learn from each other and to experiment with new ideas and ways of working will be highly advantageous.

At a team meeting, work with your team for an hour on the nature of the interface with the rest of the organisation. Highlight the type and quality of relationships and other factors which would affect your ability to change practice. What resources/skills/knowledge are there within the organisation which would support the changes you are trying to achieve? How can your learning be of benefit to the organisation too? You may choose to create a Team ECOMAP together (see Figure 2 for an example of a blank ECOMAP).

What other policies/practice initiatives are being introduced which have relevance to children and possible learning and implications for refocusing practice. For example, what is happening about the introduction of Department of Health's *Looking After Children: Assessing outcomes in child care* materials 'LAC system'(HMSO, 1995). Is your organisation adopting framework for the audit and planning for children looked after as set out in The Dartington Research Unit's *Matching Needs and Services: The audit and planning of provision for children looked after by local authorities* (Dartington Research Unit, 1995)? What is happening to implement the children's services plans? Can the potential offered by children's services plans being mandatory, inter-agency and updated annually benefit the changes you are trying to introduce?

Understanding your organisation's financial management systems is a necessary, if somewhat daunting, task. As well as trying to get to grips with the existing systems and processes, you may find opportunities to influence developments. You could for example, in a management meeting, draw attention to the inhibiting nature of current budget structures and processes, highlighting the need for more flexible budgets. You could point to developments elsewhere, for example Waltham Forest's attempts to restructure budgets to underpin a family support policy.

Waltham Forest's family support policy

Waltham Forest introduced a family support policy and strategy, intended to create a range of flexible services to support children in need and their families, which would be accessible to families and front-line staff.

The proposed action plan to support the policy includes:

- Redesignation of private and voluntary or foster care placement budgets as the family support budget.

- Placing accountability for the budget with staff who assess family needs and commission services.

- Transfer resources, as available, into individual social work teams.

Pay special attention to those who are trying to do something similar. There may be opportunities for linking up, learning from and helping each other.

Focus on strengths and opportunities, be aware of the blocks and the threats and find ways of turning these into potential supports, rather than expending all your energy fighting 'resistance'.

Figure 2 - Example of ECOMAP

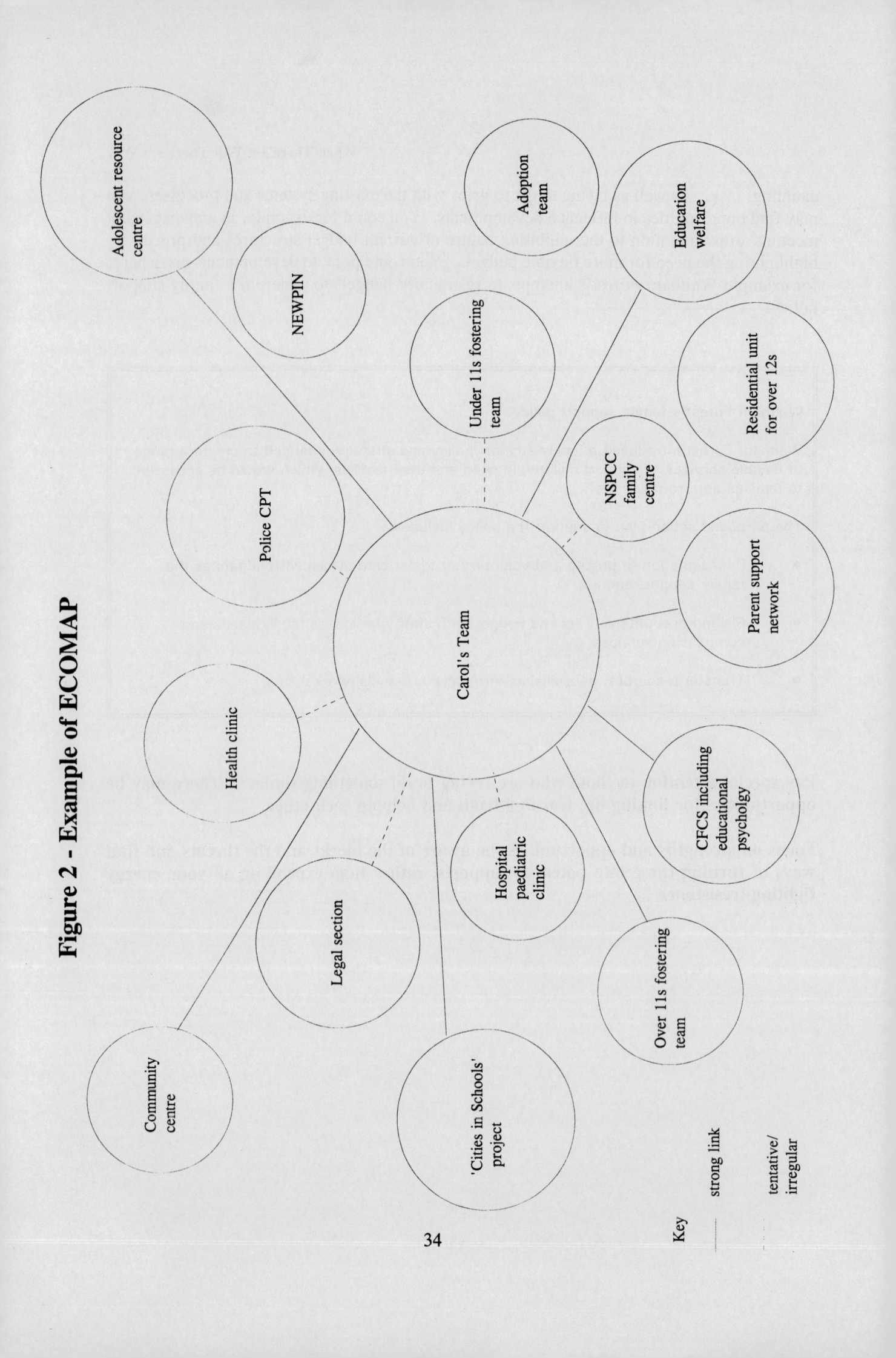

- Adolescent resource centre
- NEWPIN
- Adoption team
- Education welfare
- Under 11s fostering team
- Residential unit for over 12s
- Police CPT
- NSPCC family centre
- Carol's Team
- Parent support network
- Health clinic
- CFCS including educational psychology
- Legal section
- Hospital paediatric clinic
- Community centre
- 'Cities in Schools' project
- Over 11s fostering team

Key
——— strong link
- - - - tentative/irregular

Continuing Joan's Story

Joan's team, six weeks after the initial team day, had a vision they owned and an initial action plan. This was largely concerned with sharing and gathering information, in effect working in the interfaces, to test out their ideas. They had begun to involve others very early on in the process.

They learnt that other teams in their area were keen to hear more about recent developments and to debate the issues. Joan's team agreed to take the lead in the morning session for the next area training day, seeing this as a useful opportunity for awareness raising and for enlisting support.

The training day's programme started with a shortened version of the quiz in Appendix 3; highlighted the findings summarised in *Child Protection: Messages from Research* (Bullock 1995); gave practitioners the chance to reflect on the implications for practice; and presented some of the trends and developments presented in *Children still in Need* (NCH Action for Children 1996). Joan's team focused in particular on family group conferences, one of the features of their vision, which stimulated a rich, if at times heated debate. The team was satisfied that they had stimulated interest in the model, and had gained support for further exploration of its potential through surveying available research and making contact with those in other authorities with direct experience.

Interfacing with your community(ies)

The message here, as it is throughout, is the need to begin with an audit of what is known, and what mechanisms already exist which could be used to progress ideas before setting up new and elaborate ones.

The concept of community is a complex and controversial one. Communities are not necessarily neighbourhoods nor are they necessarily homogeneous. For these purposes we are referring to communities defined by locality and Communities of Interest. Communities of Interest are those born from common experience, for example race, religion, disability or work. Communities defined by locality can have within them many sub-communities, including Communities of Interest. It is important to find out how local people define their community.

To engage the team in working in this Interface spend an hour, at a team meeting, on:

'The community(ies) we work with - what do we know about them and who are key contacts and 'gatekeepers' to different groups and resources?'
Remember some team members may live in the community the team works in. Use their expert local knowledge.

As a way of dealing with the issues and concerns about definitions, you may choose to begin

with five minutes of initial thoughts and brief discussion of:
'What community means to me'.

Note the existing contacts. Use these to begin to test out ideas, to share and gather information.

Note where there are key contacts to be established, who will be essential to achieving the vision, and agree a strategy for following these through.

Interface with children and families

Where there are existing systems for gathering user views, use these. If they are limited to particular groups/events, for example child protection conferences, you will need to look at other mechanisms.

If there are no existing mechanisms you could look at the option of commissioning an independent person, for example, someone from a college or from a voluntary organisation, to sit in the reception area to ask users a few key questions.

Questions for users

- Did you get the help/service/advice you needed?

- What did you find most helpful about the help/service/advice received?

- What did you find least helpful?

- How could it be improved?

- If a friend/relation had a similar problem to you would you recommend that they come here?

- Could you make a contribution to increasing support to children and families locally?

Alternatively or in addition you can carry out a user survey. (See Appendix 6 for an example.)

If these options are either not feasible in the short to medium term or fail to make an impact, then seek out the views of current service users in group settings such as family centres.

It is helpful to know the views of potential users through, for example, meeting with parents and children aged eight to eleven years using the 'after school' group for children with disabilities or users of Home Start or children/young people in a pupil referral unit to get their views.

This is an area which will need to be reviewed and developed throughout. Teams and workers will be starting from very different bases, and will have to judge what is a

When There's a Will There's a Way

reasonable target. If the team lacks the confidence/skill to talk outside of their usual role, such as child protection work, with members of the public they may want to engage the help of others, perhaps from the voluntary sector.

Once users know you are interested in their views, leave a hardback exercise book in the reception area, well labelled, to show you are still interested in hearing views. You may wish to include the following or similar message in your label:
'Your views matter to us...write or draw them here, or call us on...'

6. Implementing the vision/planning the action

Practice development is a dynamic process and elements of the vision will be realised before your formal implementation date. A formal plan is still necessary as it ensures that outcomes are considered and kept in focus, and that time-scales are set and progress reviewed. This team action plan should be reviewed and revised at reasonable intervals.

The initial action plan should have a time-scale of about three months, at which point there should be a further team day, to work on implementation.

In preparation for the second team day, team meetings should be used to share information and highlight issues as they arise; reviewing the vision; logging the changes anticipated and reviewing the skills map. This is necessary if the day is to be a productive one.

The day should then be spent spelling out in detail the implementation plan specifying objectives, tasks, lead personnel, time-scales and review systems. Measures will need to be devised which will tell the team they have progressed and that the changes are making a positive difference to the experiences of children and families.

Team members can apply their energy, knowledge and creativity in mapping out ways of ensuring the continued support and involvement of key people. Methods ranging from posters and leaflets through to more formal consultations to give updates and get feedback can be used. Depending on the nature of the planned changes, workshops and seminars may be useful for dissemination of ideas.

Teams need to make sure that people consulted know how their views have been taken into account and how the information gathered has informed the plan.

Continuing Joan's story

On their follow-up team day, Joan's team identified three key objectives.

1. Their long term objective, but one which they needed to start work on immediately, was that of working more closely with communities to get better information about needs, and to be more proactive in enhancing and developing support networks. They decided to seek some external input on this as their knowledge and skills in this area needed a substantial boost.

They had already begun the work through the process of making contact and sharing ideas with key individuals and groups during the earlier phase.

2. A second objective was to establish a group for the parents of primary school children who were at risk of exclusion. A number of parents has sought help from social services and

When There's a Will There's a Way

some had already raised the question of 'care'. The parents' group would provide support, and at the same time give a parents' perspective of what interventions would be helpful to them and their children. The team hoped that in time they could facilitate a meeting between these parents, and key managers from social services and education. Initial soundings had been reasonably positive, and the team member with the teaching background agreed to take a lead, with another team member providing assistance.

3. Further exploration of the family group conferences model was their third objective as this had generated a lot of interest. They were keen but recognised the need to learn from experience in the field. This suggested a need for careful planning, training and general awareness raising across agencies and hierarchies.

7. Sustaining the process

Some ideas to help to see you through

1. Continue to encourage and prioritise practice-based discussion and skills development.

2. Use some team meetings for mini-training and awareness raising sessions. Perhaps agree to do this once every month, when business would be suspended, and information circulated or communicated in written form. To sustain the impetus requires energy and structure. Avoid the trap of collecting a list of issues to add to the forward agenda.

3. Related to the above is the need to create an informative environment for example through the circulation of summarised research and other relevant materials. ('Highlights' - a series of up-to-date summaries of key research findings covering a range of issues of relevance to professionals is available from the National Children's Bureau). Having a library, using tapes or videos to stimulate discussions and having a system whereby team members read specific articles or reports to review them and lead discussions on key points will all help. If these are plotted into team meetings or other team slots, then they need not take up extra time and with a team of six (include yourself) you could agree to approximately two each per year.

4. Some teams have an expectation that others feed back from training courses. Setting aside half an hour for more detailed feedback to try out ideas with the group, as well as circulating information would help others to benefit from training and the worker to transfer learning into the work place. On team days you could build in a couple of slots for workers to share an exercise or a new skill they have learnt or a game that has been bought for working with children. These can be very good team building exercises, which at the same time serve the purpose of disseminating learning. (See Appendix 2 for suggested programmes for team days.)

5. Some teams have a practice of sharing how they are feeling at the beginning of a team meeting. You could add to or have an alternative form of sharing information where team members are asked to share for example *'One new thing I have learnt about my work this week is...'; 'I am about to start a course on...'; 'At the moment I am working mainly on...'* (See Hearn, B, Darvill, G and Morris, B, 1992, for more information and ideas.)

6. Whatever team exchange and practice development systems you establish, be sure to review them on a regular basis.

7. Find training events which are likely to enhance the developments. You could try getting on a few mailing lists for direct information for example National Children's Bureau, Family Rights Group.

8. Establish mutual supervisory/mentor links within and/or beyond the team. You may be working in an office with another team leader with whom you should ideally be working more closely, but something has always got in the way. Use this opportunity to get on track.

9. In moving beyond the team to test out your ideas you may have made contact with someone dealing with or who has dealt with a similar problem. Try linking up. Meeting together may not be easy but can always telephone and, if your agency is IT friendly, you can keep in touch and encourage each other using e-mail and voice-mail.

10. The change you are trying to achieve may require action across agencies, and there may be some multi-agency training at the outset. As part of your action plan for taking the learning back into the work place how about setting up a cross-agency learning set?

What if it doesn't work/goes wrong?

Despite giving it your best shot, it may still fail to refocus the work of your team. In examining what went wrong look at the list of factors which support and those which inhibit, detailed in the preface, and see which might apply to your situation. Reflect on Smale's fallacies, and review how much these apply in your situation. And remember the wise words attributed to Rita Mae Brown, 'Insanity is doing the same thing over and over again and expecting different results' (Bill O'Hanlon, *Creating Possibilities* seminar, Institute for Child Health, London 11 November 1993)

And finally...

Expect euphoria, frustration, pain, and relapses before the change embeds, and then it is time for the next journey.

Figure 3 - Representation of the process

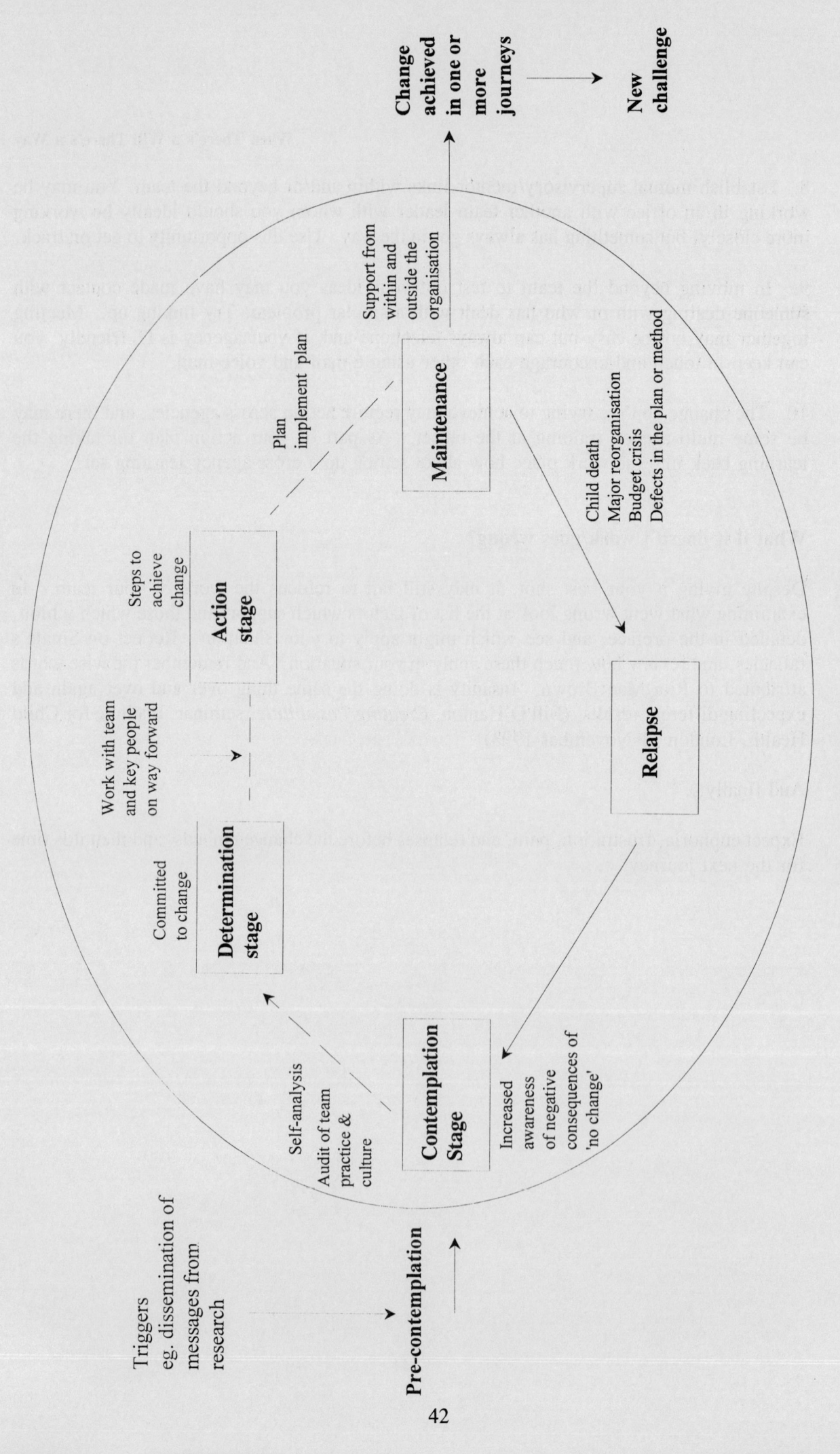

Pre-contemplation →

Triggers eg. dissemination of messages from research

Contemplation Stage
- Self-analysis
- Audit of team practice & culture

Determination stage
- Committed to change
- Work with team and key people on way forward

Action stage
- Steps to achieve change
- Plan implement plan

Maintenance
- Support from within and outside the organisation

Relapse
- Child death
- Major reorganisation
- Budget crisis
- Defects in the plan or method
- Increased awareness of negative consequences of 'no change'

Change achieved in one or more journeys → **New challenge**

Based on Prochaska & Diclemente's *Six Cycles of Change*

Figure 4 - Representation of process

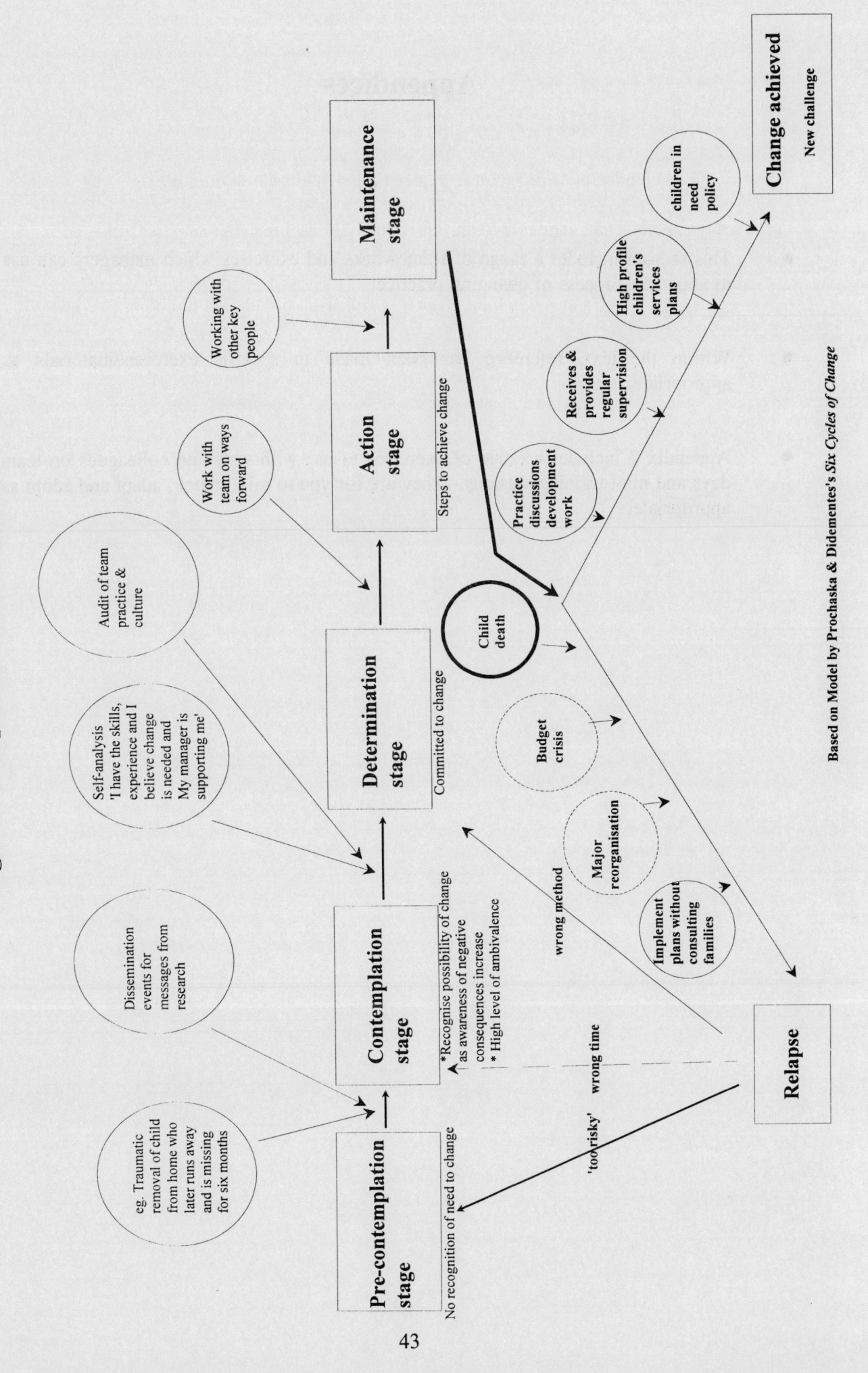

Pre-contemplation stage — No recognition of need to change

- eg. Traumatic removal of child from home who later runs away and is missing for six months

Contemplation stage
- *Recognise possibility of change as awareness of negative consequences increase
- *High level of ambivalence

- Dissemination events for messages from research

Determination stage — Committed to change

- Self-analysis 'I have the skills, experience and I believe change is needed and My manager is supporting me'
- Audit of team practice & culture

Action stage — Steps to achieve change

- Work with team on ways forward

Maintenance stage

- Working with other key people
- Practice discussions development work
- Receives & provides regular supervision
- High profile children's services plans
- children in need policy

Change achieved — New challenge

Relapse
- 'too risky'
- wrong time
- wrong method
- Implement plans without consulting families
- Major reorganisation
- Budget crisis
- Child death

Based on Model by Prochaska & Didemente's *Six Cycles of Change*

43

Appendices

- This section includes a range of frameworks and exercises which managers can use to assist the process of changing practice.

- Within the text, reference has been made to specific exercises/materials as appropriate.

- Appendix 7 includes a range of exercises to use with staff and colleagues on team days and mini-training sessions. They are for you to mix, match, adapt and adopt as appropriate.

Appendix 1

Adapted from: McCormack, T (1989) *Approaches to Family and Community Development*, Dublin

Once upon a time there was a small village on the edge of a river. The people there were good and life in the village was good. One day a villager noticed a baby floating down the river. The villager quickly jumped into the river and swam out to save the baby from drowning. The next day the same villager was walking along the river bank and noticed two babies in the river. He called for help, and both babies were rescued from the swift waters. The following day four babies were seen caught in the turbulent waters. Then eight, then more and still more. The villagers organised themselves quickly, setting up watchtowers and training teams of swimmers who could resist the swift waters and rescue babies. Rescue squads were soon working 24 hours a day. Each day the numbers of babies floating down the river increased. While not all the babies, now very numerous, could be saved, the villagers felt they were doing well to save as many as they could each day. Indeed the village priest blessed them for their good work. Life in the village continued on this basis. One day, however, someone raised the question, *'But where are all the babies coming from? Who is throwing them into the river? Why? Let's organise a team to go upstream and see who is doing it'*. The village leaders countered with *'And if we go upstream who will operate the rescue service? We need every concerned person here'*. 'But don't you see', cried one lone voice, *'if we find out who is throwing the babies in we can stop the problem and no babies will drown? By going upstream we can eliminate the cause of the problem'*. *'It is too risky'*. So the numbers of babies in the river increased daily. Those saved increased but those who drowned increased even more.

Appendix 2

Programmes for team days

General preparation for any team day

- Early preparation includes securing agreement of own manager, sorting out cover, agreeing date and booking appropriate venue.
- Agree agenda with the team well in advance.
- Agree what needs to be done and who needs to do it at least two weeks ahead.
- Agree how and who will facilitate/lead the day.
- Circulate all relevant reading articles at least ten days ahead.
- Agree lunch and break arrangements.

Programme A

Theme: *Messages from Research*: the implications for our practice.

Preparation

Agree which team member will share learning about a particular method/idea/skill

Circulate the summary by Michael Little and Carolyn Davies (1995) 'Family Circle', *Community Care,* No.1073 (22 June) pp.18-19

- Look through exercise on 'Criteria for decision-making' (Appendix 7f), and see what preparation is suggested, for example cases to be selected in advance, reading conclusions of *Messages from Research*.

- Select ten questions from the quiz/add your own.

The day

09.30   Warm-up

      a) Things I need to leave behind to get the most from the day
      or;
      b) One good thing that has happened to me in the past week, and one not so good thing
      or;
      c) What I will contribute to make today a worthwhile experience.

This page may be photocopied for use within your organisation. © National Children's Bureau

09.45	The quiz
	Answers and discussion
10.15	Team exercise
	Response to research findings and conclusions (see Appendix 7a for exercise)
11.00	BREAK
11.15	Exercise: Criteria for decision-making (Appendix 7f)
12.45	LUNCH
13.45	Team members share knowledge/skill/information
14.00	Family support (team discussion)
	Fears and anxieties Hopes Benefits and demands
14.30	Defining family support (see exercise in Appendix 7i)
15.00	BREAK
15.15	In relation to family support and child protection work (team discussion):
	What do we do well...according to whom? What we are not so good at...according to whom?
16.00	Team plan
	What do we need to do next? Prioritise at least three things. When will we do it? Who will take the lead? How will we make sure that we do it?
16.45	END
NOTE:	This programme assumes six-ten participants. If there are more than ten or less than six than adjustments will be necessary, for example less small group work for lower number and longer time/different approach for information sharing if higher.

This page may be photocopied for use within your organisation. © National Children's Bureau

When there's a will there's a way

Programme B

Theme: Developing practice to support families and protect children, our ways forward

Preparation

Find appropriate senior manager to give an overview of national and local developments.

Circulate Burton's summary of Hearn (1995) *Child Family Support and Protection* (Appendix 7i)

The day

9.30   Senior manager gives overview

Team discussion

10.15 Team exercise.

Use the 'miracle question' to help the team project into the future:

'Imagine that tonight when you are asleep there is a miracle, but as you are asleep you don't know it is happening. When you wake up, two years will have gone by and the team will be practising in a way which fits with your ideas on supporting families and protecting children. What will be the first sign that things have changed? What will you see happening? How will team members be behaving/how will families be responding/who will be the first to notice the changes in practice?'

Help the team to keep focused on what will be happening, when they identify things which won't be happening, ask what will be happening instead?

Log all ideas on flip-chart

Group discussion of similarities, differences and contradictions.

11.15 BREAK

11.30 Practices from the future vision which the team does now.

How will the team sustain these?

12.00 Practice(s) which team has to develop or change

This page may be photocopied for use within your organisation. © National Children's Bureau

List all areas
Prioritise three for action

12.30 LUNCH

13.30 Warm-up

'Walking the scales' exercise (see Appendix 7n)

13.45 Action plan for developing and changing practice

What, who, with whom, by when?

15.00 BREAK

15.15 What we need and from whom to help us achieve changes.

16.30 END

When there's a will there's a way

Programme C

Theme: Working in partnership

Preparation

Circulate article on Family Group Conferences, Hirst, J (1996) *'Family planning'*, *Community Care*, no.1119, (9 May) pp.16-17.

Circulate the summary of the research by Thoburn, Lewis & Shemmings *'Paternalism or Partnership? Family Involvement in the child protection process'*, in Bullock, R and others (1995) *Child Protection: Messages from Research*. HMSO, pp.85-87.

Adapt exercise on Partnership in Appendix 7c of this guide

The day

9.30   Warm-up: Things about myself

Team members should note in the four corners of a sheet of paper four things about themselves, three true and one false. Talk to someone else, whose task is to find out which is false. When they do swap around, and then pair up with someone else. Exercise continues for no more than 15 minutes.

10.00   Exercise on partnership and participation from Appendix 7c of this guide.

11.00   BREAK

11.15   Discussion of article on family group conferences
Information exchange - What is happening locally about this? What more do we need to know? Is it right for us? What problems might be involved?

11.45   Discussion of summary of Thoburn et al's research

Pool ideas on 'key messages for practice' from Materials and Exercise.

12.30   LUNCH

This page may be photocopied for use within your organisation.   © National Children's Bureau

13.30 ECOMAP of team links and relationships

Where is partnership well developed? How do we know? With whom do we need to improve on partnership work?

Prioritise three key relationships/links to work on.

15.00 BREAK

15.15 Individual goal setting. Use 'Walking the scale' (Appendix 7n).

15.30 Team action plan

16.30 END

When there's a will there's a way

Programme D

Theme: The needs of children and families in the community(ies)

Preparation

- Distribute copy of Gill's article 'Neighbourhood watch' from *Community Care* 8 June 1995, pp.30-31

- Distribute the Executive Summary of Audit Commission Report, *'Seen but not Heard'* (Audit Commission, 1994)

- Get hold of the authority's current children's services plan.

- Have available copy of the children in need policy/any other guidance produced by the authority.

- Look over and adapt the exercise on 'Defining, prioritising and measuring needs' in Appendix 7l.

The day

09.30 Warm-up - 'Problem free talk', in pairs. Find out as much as possible about strengths, interests, hobbies and skills of the other person.

09.45 ECOMAP of team links and relationships.

- What needs to be done to maintain or change these;
- Clear gaps;
- How to address.

11.00 BREAK

11.15 Working with communities

- Five minutes noting team's initial thoughts on 'What community means to me'.
- Exercise in two groups on 'Community support for families' in Appendix 7k.
- Whole team discussion.

This page may be photocopied for use within your organisation. © National Children's Bureau

12.30 LUNCH

13.30 'Walking the scale'. Exercise in Appendix 7n.

13.45 Issues from the articles and material circulated.

14.00 Exercise on 'Defining and prioritising needs' Parts I and II (Appendix 7l).

15.00 BREAK

15.15 Exercise continued

16.00 What next?

16.30 END

This page may be photocopied for use within your organisation. © National Children's Bureau

Appendix 3a

Quiz for team leaders and practitioners
To identify gaps in knowledge and to assess knowledge acquired through the development process

When/how to use

a) In full at the beginning and end of a training/development activity
b) Select ten or so questions to use at the start of a team day/practice discussion slot.
c) To be done 'unseen' or to be taken away for research with set time.

Legislation

1. Section 17 of Part III of the Children Act states that 'it shall be the general duty of every local authority to safeguard and promote the welfare of children within their area who are in need.'

    - What is meant by local authority?

    - How is 'in need' defined.

    - There are two parts to the general duty, what is part (b)?

2. List as many of the duties and powers outlined in Part I of Schedule 2 of the Act.

3. List the range of possible support services specified in Schedule 2? For whom should such services be provided?

This page may be photocopied for use within your organisation. © National Children's Bureau

When there's a will there's a way

4. What is the main concern of Part V of the Act. What is your understanding of Section 47?

5. How and where does the Act state the explicit inter-agency responsibilities in the provision of family support services?

6. When does the local authority have a duty to consider the racial groups to which children in need in their area belong?

7. When undertaking assessments of children with disabilities, which other Acts will have to be considered?

8. What did the Audit Commission see as a key requirement for improved coordination of services to children in need?

This page may be photocopied for use within your organisation. © National Children's Bureau

When there's a will there's a way

Research on placements and outcomes for children

Please note that the term 'care' is used here because this was the relevant term at the time that the research was done in the mid-late 1980s.

9. Bebbington and Miles (1989) in a study of 2,500 children admitted to care, compiled the following table which compares the probability of admission for two children in similar circumstances.

Consider the profiles and select the most likely odds for their admission to care:

Child A - Aged 5-9	Child B - Aged 5-9
• No dependence on social security benefits	• Household head receives income support
• Two-parent family	• Single adult household
• Three or fewer children	• Four or more children
• White	• Mixed ethnic origin
• Owner-occupied home	• Privately rented home
• More rooms than people	• One or more persons per room
Odds	*Odds*
1 in 10; 1 in 50; 1 in 100; 1 in 1,000; 1 in 3,000; 1 in 7,000; 1 in 10,000	*1 in 10; 1 in 50; 1 in 100; 1 in 1,000; 1 in 3,000; 1 in 7,000; 1 in 10,000*

10. What is the period after which a child's stay, when being looked after by a local authority is likely to become a long or very long one?

11. What have researchers both here and in the USA identified as the 'key to discharge'?

12. Which of the following groups of children are likely to have the following experiences of the care system:

The children	The experience
• Asian children?	• over-represented in the care system?
• pre-school and five-to-ten year old African and African-Caribbean?	• under-represented in the care system?
• African teenagers?	• more likely to experience multiple admissions?
• children of mixed parentage?	• more likely to experience placement breakdowns?

13. Survey data from the mid-late 1980s indicated that there were:

    • *more/fewer* admissions of black children to care? Delete as appropriate.

    • admissions for 'temporary care' were *more/less* common for young African-Caribbean and African children that for any other group? (Delete as appropriate.)

14. The proportion of children who leave care between 16-18 years and eventually return to their families is?

    1/10; 1/5; 2/5; 3/5.

15. **True or false** (where false, note the correct answer)

    • Once a young person leaving care gets his/her own flat he/she tend to remain there for two or three years.

    • One in seven of young women leaving care at 18 are already pregnant.

    • Research by Stein & Carey (1986) found that 25 per cent of young people leaving care had five or more placements.

This page may be photocopied for use within your organisation. © National Children's Bureau

When there's a will there's a way

- The unemployment figures for young people leaving care are roughly equivalent to local averages.

- The ex-care population is heavily over-represented by the homeless and destitute young people in major cities.

- Section 24 of the Children Act 1989 lays a duty on local authorities to:

    '**advise, assist and befriend**' care leavers aged 16-21, **AND** to provide assistance '**in kind, or in exceptional circumstances, in cash**'.

16. What proportion of placement moves did Berridge and Cleaver (1987) attribute to administrative inconvenience or as part of the planning process?

17. What percentage of children and adolescents taken away from their families into the care of a local authority eventually return home?

    - What percentage return home before six months?

    - What percentage return home within the first week?

Family support

18. The Audit Commission in its report, *Seen but not Heard* (1994), made a number of recommendations for moving forward in relation to family support work. What were they?

19. Gibbons & Thorpe (1989) carried out a comparative study of families receiving Home Start services in one centre with families allocated to social workers for preventive work. Home Start is a voluntary sector project which uses matched volunteers to provide support to individual families. Because the study was concentrated on one centre the findings have to be treated with caution, although centres do follow a similar pattern of service delivery. Which of the following are TRUE or FALSE findings?

    - Home Start was working predominantly with 'ordinary families' under temporary pressure with only an insignificant minority of vulnerable families facing severe difficulties.

This page may be photocopied for use within your organisation. © National Children's Bureau

When there's a will there's a way

- On the whole social workers made more home visits to individual families than the Home Start volunteers.

- Home Start users were more satisfied with the service they received than those receiving social work support.

Child protection research

20. What were the five pre-conditions of effective practice to protect children identified in the recent publication *Child Protection: Messages from Research*?

21. What percentage of children dealt with through the child protection process remain at home with their families?

22. For what percentage of family members did Thoburn et al consider that the potential for full partnership in the child protection process had been achieved in the first six months?

23. What percentage of cases are filtered out of the child protection process before reaching a case conference, according to the findings of Gibbons et al?

24. How long on average did the Bristol researchers, Farmer and Owen, find professionals spending on the construction of a protection plan at case conferences?

25. The researchers expressed a concern over the relationship between child protection and family support. How would you summarise this concern to one of your staff?

This page may be photocopied for use within your organisation. © National Children's Bureau

Appendix 3b

Answers to questionnaire for team leaders

1. - 'Local authority' in England and Wales means the council of a county, a metropolitan district, a London Borough or the Common Council of the City of London.

   - 'In need' is defined in Section 17 (10). There are three elements to the definition:

   i) The child is unlikely to achieve or maintain, or to have the opportunity of achieving or maintaining, a reasonable standard of health or development without the provision for the child of services by a local authority under this part of the act; **or**

   ii) The child's health or development is likely to be significantly impaired, or further impaired, without provision for the child of such services; **or**

   iii) The child is disabled.

   - Part b of the general duty is: so far as is consistent with that duty (safeguard and promote welfare), to promote the upbringing of such children by their families, by providing a range and level of services appropriate to those children's needs.

2. Duties and powers in Part I of Section 2:

   - identification of children in need; publish information about services provided; ensure that information gets to those who might benefit; open and maintain a register of disabled children; assessment of children's needs; prevention of neglect and abuse; provision of accommodation in order to protect child; provision for disabled children to minimise the effect of their disabilities and to give them opportunities to lead lives which are as normal as possible; provision to reduce need to bring care proceedings; provision for children living with their families; family centres; maintenance of family home to enable child who is not living at home to return or to maintain contact; duty to consider racial groups to which children in need belong.

3. - advice, guidance and counselling;
   occupational, cultural, or recreational facilities;
   home help, including laundry facilities;
   assistance to enable the child or family to have a holiday;
   facilities for, or assisting with, travelling to and from home to take advantage

This page may be photocopied for use within your organisation. © National Children's Bureau

of a particular service;
family centres;
assisting an adult who has ill-treated, or may ill-treat a child living at the same premises to move out.

- services should be provided for children in need and their families.

4. Part V is primarily concerned with the protection of children.

    Section 47 is about a local authority's duty to investigate. The actual wording in the Act is 'make enquiries':

    'Where a local authority has reasonable cause to suspect that a child is suffering or is likely to suffer, significant harm, the authority shall make (or cause to be made) such enquiries as they consider necessary to enable them to decide whether they should take any action to safeguard or promote the child's welfare. The enquiries shall, in particular, be directed towards establishing whether the authority should...exercise any of their other powers under the Act'.

5. Part II Section 27.

6. When recruiting day carers or foster carers; also must ensure that day care provision meets additional needs of children that arise from their racial origin or cultural and linguistic background; in addition LAs are duty bound to provide relevant cultural activities as part of their family support services.

7. Chronically sick and disabled persons Act 1970; the Education Act 1981; and the Disabled Persons (Services, Consultation and Representation) Act 1986.

8. The development of a joint strategy in the form of a (mandatory) children's services plan.

9. Child A: 1 in 7,000; Child B: 1 in 10.

10. Six weeks

11. Contact with their parents and other family members. Contact is defined widely and includes visits, telephone calls and letters.

12. See attached diagram.

This page may be photocopied for use within your organisation. © National Children's Bureau

Figure 5 - Information relevant to Question 12

Ethnic origin of children admitted to care 1985-87

Over the two years 3748 children had 4682 admissions between them. The first pie chart below shows the distribution of children across all ethnic groups. The second shows more clearly how the black children in our sample are distributed between minority ethnic groups

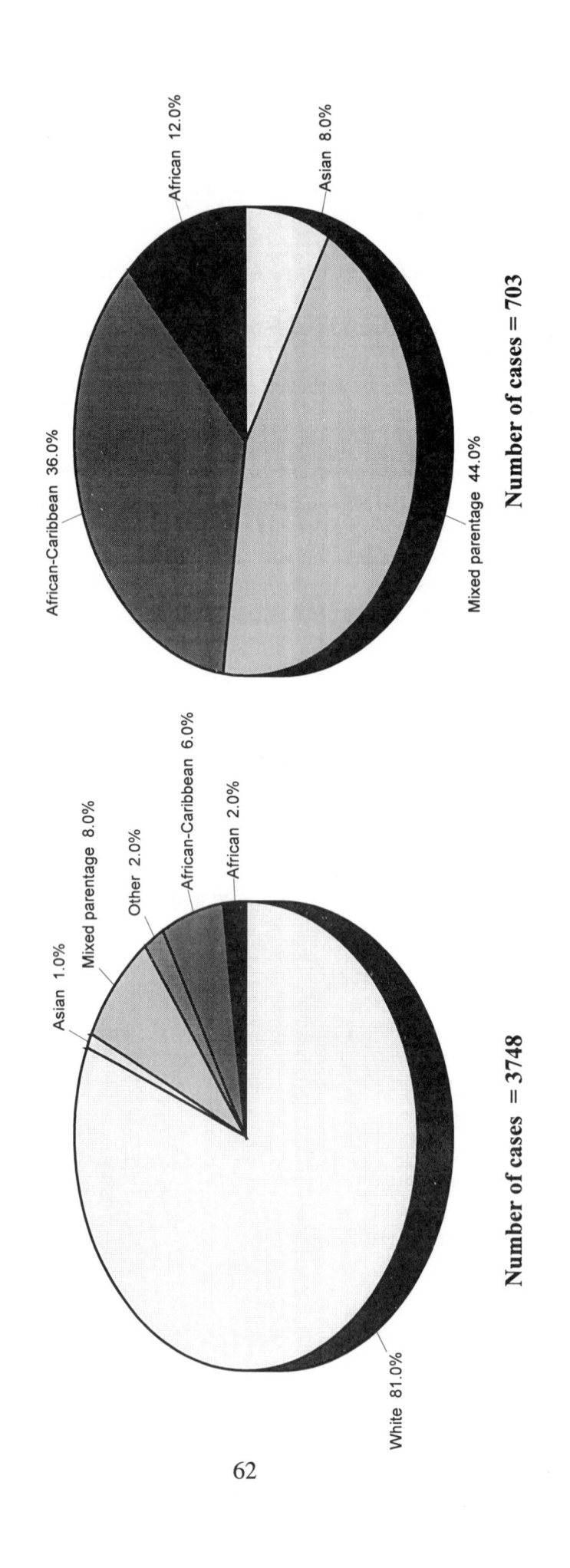

![Pie chart 1: White 81.0%, Asian 1.0%, Mixed parentage 8.0%, Other 2.0%, African-Caribbean 6.0%, African 2.0%. Number of cases = 3748]

![Pie chart 2: African 12.0%, Asian 8.0%, Mixed parentage 44.0%, African-Caribbean 36.0%. Number of cases = 703]

Rowe et al. 'Child Care Now' in Department of Health (1991) *Patterns & Outcomes in Child Placement: Messages from Current Research & their Implications*

i) Pre-school and five- to ten-year-old year old African and African-Caribbean children; African teenagers and children of mixed parentage are over-represented in the care system, with children of mixed parentage, grossly so.

ii) Asian children are under-represented.

iii) Children of mixed parentage are more likely to experience multiple admissions.

iv) Children of mixed parentage are also more likely to experience placement breakdown.

13. • There are fewer compulsory admissions of black children to care (pre Children Act research).

    • Admissions with the aim of 'temporary care' are much more common for young African-Caribbean and African children than for any other group.

14. • Two out of every five children who leave care between 16 and 18 years old eventually return to their families.

15. i) **FALSE** Generally young people seem to move around between bedsits, parents, friends and are often 'semi-homeless'. Garnett in one study (1992), found that out of 15 young people whose last placement was a flat, and whose whereabouts were known two years later, only three were still living at home.

    ii) **TRUE** 1 in 7 young women leaving care at 18 was already pregnant (Garnett 1992).

    iii) **FALSE** Not 25 per cent but 40 per cent of young people leaving care had had five or more placements.

    iv) **FALSE** Unemployment figures for young people leaving care are consistently higher than local averages.

    v) **TRUE** Research studies have found that 25 to 40 per cent of all homeless young people under 21 have a care background. 29 per cent of all young people seen by Centre Point between April-September 1993 had a care background.

    vi) **TRUE** to first part of statement. Second part correct in spirit but the Act authorises rather than requires authorities to provide assistance in kind, or in exceptional circumstances, in cash.

16. Two thirds of placement moves were deemed by Berridge as being for administrative convenience.

This page may be photocopied for use within your organisation. © National Children's Bureau

When there's a will there's a way

17. 90 per cent of children separated from their families eventually return home; 60 per cent of children return home before six months; and 20 per cent within the first week.

    (source: Bullock, R, Little, M, and Millham, S (1993) *Going Home: the return of children separated from thier families.* Dartmouth)

18. Joint strategy in the form of children's services plans; needs-led approach; joint planning and co-ordination of family support activities; developing joint ventures; rebalancing priorities and resources in social services; evaluation of health visitors' activities.

19. i) **FALSE** Significant minority were families facing severe difficulties. They were not predominantly ordinary families under temporary pressure. Overall Home Start families were experiencing nearly as many social, economic and personal difficulties as the clients of social work departments.

    ii) **FALSE** Volunteers visited more frequently.

    iii) **TRUE**

20. Sensitive and informed professional/client relationship; achieving the right balance of power; need for wider perspective on child protection; effective supervision and training; enhancing children's general quality of life.

21. 96 per cent.

22. 3 per cent.

23. 75 per cent.

24. 9 minutes.

25. Questioned whether the balance between child protection and the range of supports and interventions available is correct and concluded that the balance between services was unsatisfactory. Concerned that the stress upon child protection investigations and not enquiries and the failure to follow through interventions with much needed family support prevented professionals from meeting the needs of children and families.

This page may be photocopied for use within your organisation. © National Children's Bureau

Appendix 4a

Agreeing the supervision contract

Make an agreement

The agreement should take the following factors into account:

- Sessions should include an appropriate balance of the different functions of supervision. It should meet both the social worker's need for development including planning, training and learning opportunities and the line manager's needs to manage;

- There should be an agreed system for reviewing and evaluating this balance;

- Sessions need to take place on a regular planned basis to meet the needs of the social worker;

- Sessions should be properly recorded;

- Explicit arrangements for reviewing and evaluating any learning objectives should be agreed and included in the supervision agreement;

- The agreement should take into account the individual needs of the worker and must address factors relating to ethnicity, gender, as well as the inherent power structure;

- Responsibility should be shared between the social worker and the supervisor for preparing for the sessions, including agreeing an agenda.

From: *Developing Good Child Protection Practice: Guidance for Managers* (unpublished) Sara Noakes, National Children's Bureau

Appendix 4b

Format for supervision contract

This is one example of a format. You may want to change it, or your agency may already have a format and/or supervision policy.

Supervision ground rules

Frequency and duration

Venue

Agenda

- How will it be set
- Content

Recording

- Method
- Purpose for which it may/may not be used
- Who else may see the record

Feedback

Arrangements for handling disagreement

How and when contract will be reviewed

Name of Supervisor: Name of Supervisee:
Signature: Signature:

Appendix 4c

Staff supervision in social care
Policies, principles and purposes

Given that the process of adult learning is fundamental to effective supervision, and that too much anxiety will block the development process, failure to address the meaning of inequality and difference will undermine the supervisory process.

Reflections

The following questions can be used to reflect on issues of ethnicity, gender, class, age, disability, sexual orientation, religion or nationality.

- As a supervisor, what feelings, fears and fantasies do you have about supervising workers from a different group?

- In what ways are you conscious of treating those workers differently, especially where issues of control arise?

- As a supervisor, what feelings, fears and fantasies do you think a worker from a different ethnic group might have about you? How do you think he/she perceives your authority?

- As a supervisor, to what extent have you tried to address these issues openly with workers?

- What provision is there in your agency for supervisory situations which become badly stuck because of ethnic differences? Are there appropriate consultants you and your workers can approach?

- What training does your agency provide to help you address this issue?

Reflections

- How would you characterise your learning history? What strengths and blocks in learning situations do you bring from this? Are any blocks related to experiences of discrimination in the learning environment?

- When do you get stuck in the learning cycle, what behaviour do you get into. Think of a recent learning experience and analyse it in terms of the learning cycle. What lessons could you learn as to how you improve your learning process?
  Common issues are:

When there's a will there's a way

- ○ Failure to take responsibility for our own learning. 'I'll just go on a course and they can teach me'.

- ○ Failure to commit the time and energy for opportunities to rehearse new skills or translate theory to practice.

- ○ Making insufficient use of colleagues or supervisors to assist us with our development either in terms of giving us critical feedback or in terms of using them as mentors/models.

- Have you discussed with the people you supervise their learning history and preferences? If not you may unintentionally trigger a block in their response to supervision, not because you have done anything wrong, but because you are unaware of the significance that a particular way of doing or saying something has for the worker. Many supervisors find that taking a learning and supervisory history can explain puzzling or ambivalent responses to supervision.

Stress management, staff support and self-care

Reflections

- What are you currently getting from your supervisor?

- Are your expectations of each other clear and agreed?

- What most needs changing in the service you receive from the person responsible for supervising you?

- Do you fear or experience your supervisor as acting in a discriminatory way towards you?

From: Morrison, T (1995) *Staff supervision in social care: an action learning approach.* Longman

Appendix 5a

P Hardiker's (1994) Social Policy Contexts of Child Welfare

Level of Intervention	Welfare Model: Role of the State			
	Last Resort	Needs-Based	Combatting Social Disadvantage	The Enabling Authority
FIRST (Populations: diversion)			Community Development	
SECOND (Early risks)		Counselling and Social Care Planning		
THIRD (serious risks)	Remedial Interventions			
FOURTH (Rehabilitation)	Planning for permanence: Damage limitation			

(Right side: CONTINUUM OF FAMILY SUPPORT SERVICES / Statutory and independent sectors/ direct and indirect collaboration)

P Hardiker's (1994) Models of Prevention in Child Care

Models of Welfare / Level of prevention	Residual	Institutional	Developmental	Radical
1. *Primary* i) action to prevent problems from arising ii) action to reduce the need for the formal services of the SSD			1. Primary/ developmental	
2. *Secondary* i) early identification of and action to resolve problems ii) intervention aimed at early restoration of non client status		2. Secondary/ Institutional		
3. *Tertiary* i) action to prevent the worst effects of chronic well established problems ii) action to prevent clients from being drawn into increasingly intrusive and damaging interventions	3. Tertiary/ residual			
4. *Quaternary* i) action to prevent damage arising from long term substitute care ii) permanency planning				

Appendix 5b

Framework for social work activity:
Smale and others, *CSW - a paradigm for change*

These illustrations provide a framework on which the activites required to work with a family or across a community can be mapped and so reflect how both support and protection are inter-dependent. The responses necessary to successfully sustain a single family with complex needs and including abuse can be mapped out using this matrix.

Figure 6

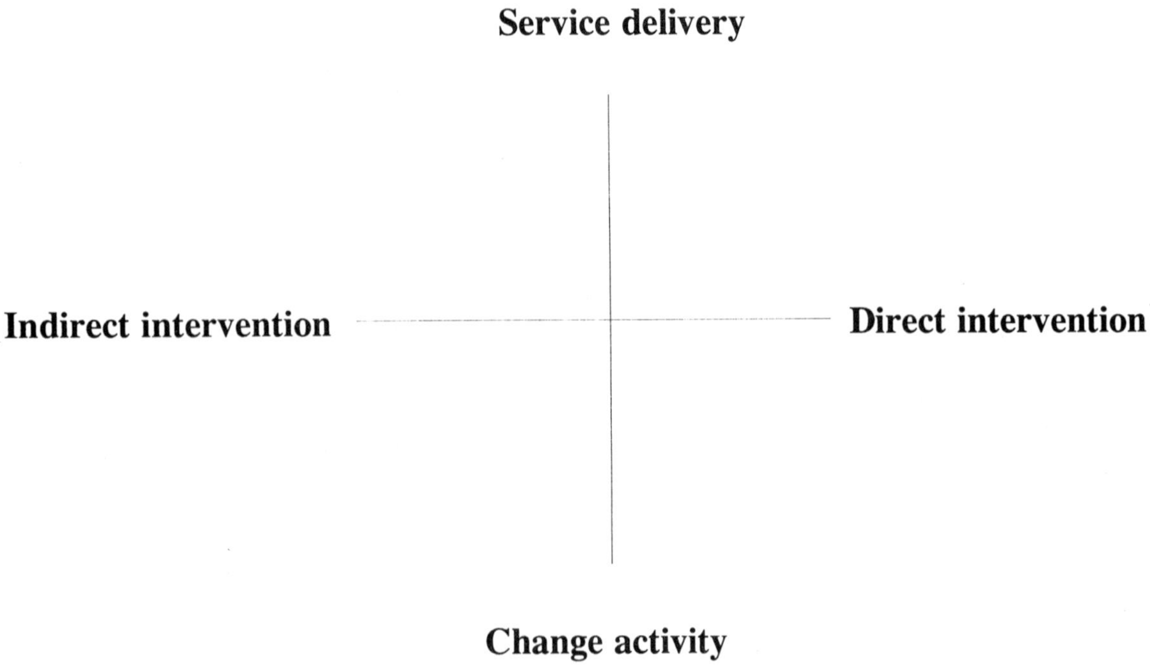

```
                    Service delivery
                          |
                          |
                          |
Indirect intervention ————+———— Direct intervention
                          |
                          |
                          |
                    Change activity
```

From: Hearn, B. (1995) *Child and Family Support and Protection: A practical approach.* National Children's Bureau

Appendix 5b

Alison, age 27 years, referred herself because she had seen the social work team members at a community festival and a local tenants dance. She had asked around about them and decided they were 'OK'.

Alison arrived at the social work office with a photo of her daughter with a split lip and detailed how she had hit her daughter. Having had a recent spell in prison, she was socially isolated living 300 miles away from her family who had rejected her because her daughter was of mixed parentage. Known to be voilent towards officials, Alison was extremely ambivalent about referring herself and her child. This diagram illustrates how activity was spread between the quadrants at the point of referral.

Figure 7

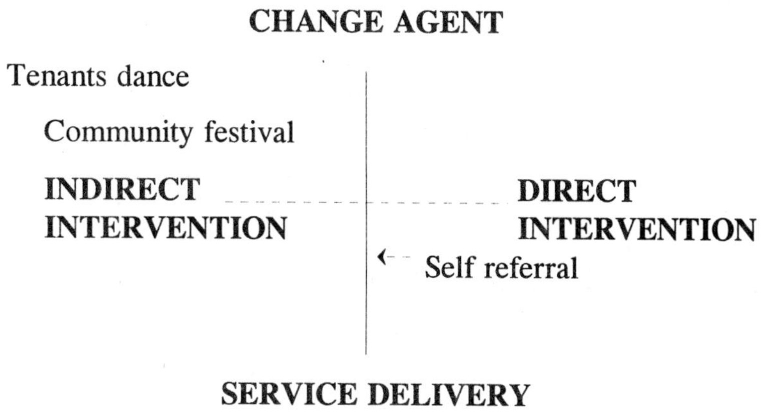

```
                    CHANGE AGENT
   Tenants dance              |
      Community festival      |
     INDIRECT          ------ | ------   DIRECT
     INTERVENTION             |          INTERVENTION
                         ← -- Self referral
                              |
                    SERVICE DELIVERY
```

From: Hearn, B. (1995) *Child and Family Support and Protection: A practical approach.* National Children's Bureau

Appendix 5b (continued)

After referral a great deal of focused work was undertaken on the right sided quadrants and reflects a typical problem of intervention. Part of the process was helping Alison to become part of the local community and contribute to it. To achieve this, work had to be undertaken in the other two quadrants

Figure 8

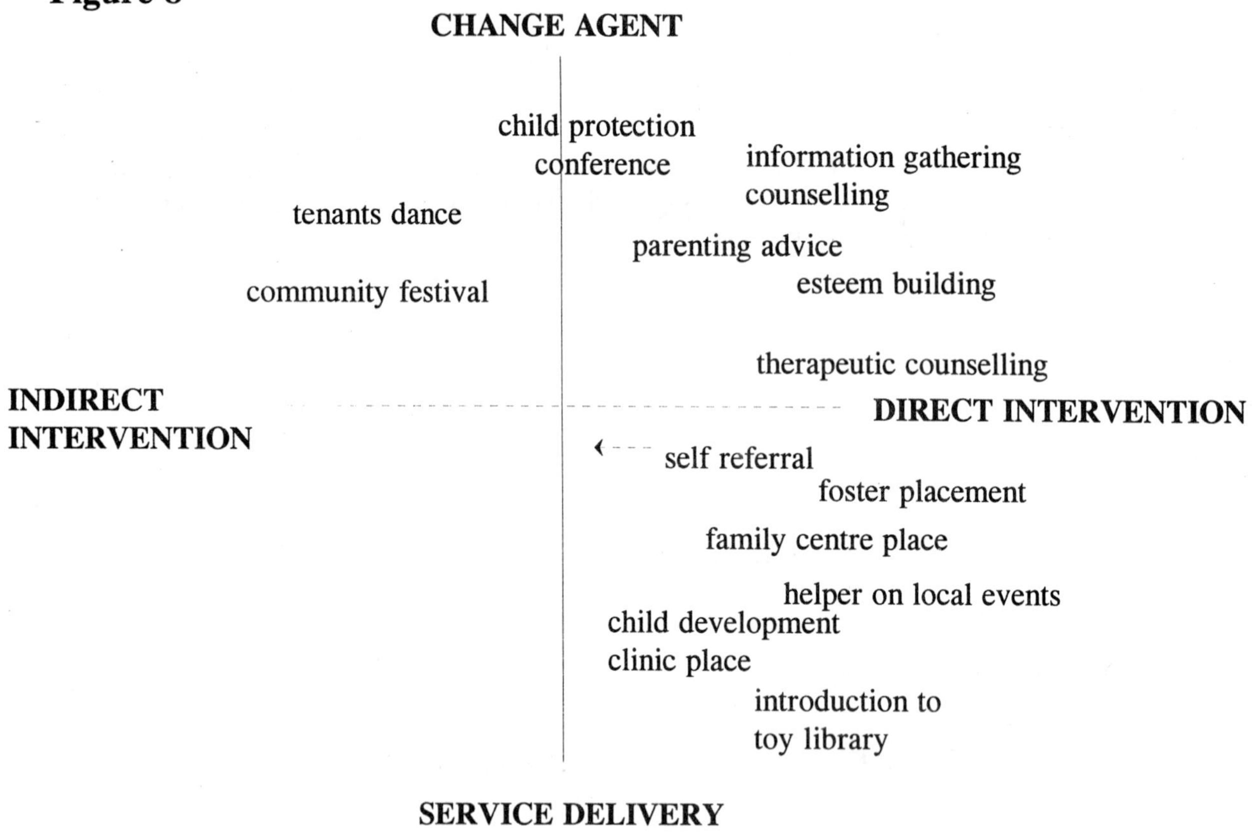

```
                          CHANGE AGENT
                               |
                  child protection
                       conference    information gathering
                                         counselling
             tenants dance
                                  parenting advice
           community festival         esteem building

                                   therapeutic counselling
INDIRECT                                          DIRECT INTERVENTION
INTERVENTION  - - - - - - - - - - - - - - - - - -
                           <- - - self referral
                                         foster placement
                                    family centre place
                                           helper on local events
                              child development
                              clinic place
                                         introduction to
                                         toy library
                               |
                         SERVICE DELIVERY
```

From: Hearn, B. (1995) *Child and Family Support and Protection: A practical approach*. National Children's Bureau

Appendix 5b (continued)

Over a three-year period Alison and her daughter, through many ups and downs, worked alongside and with the social worker team to improve her parenting skills and expand her social network. The child was protected and the family preserved.

Figure 9

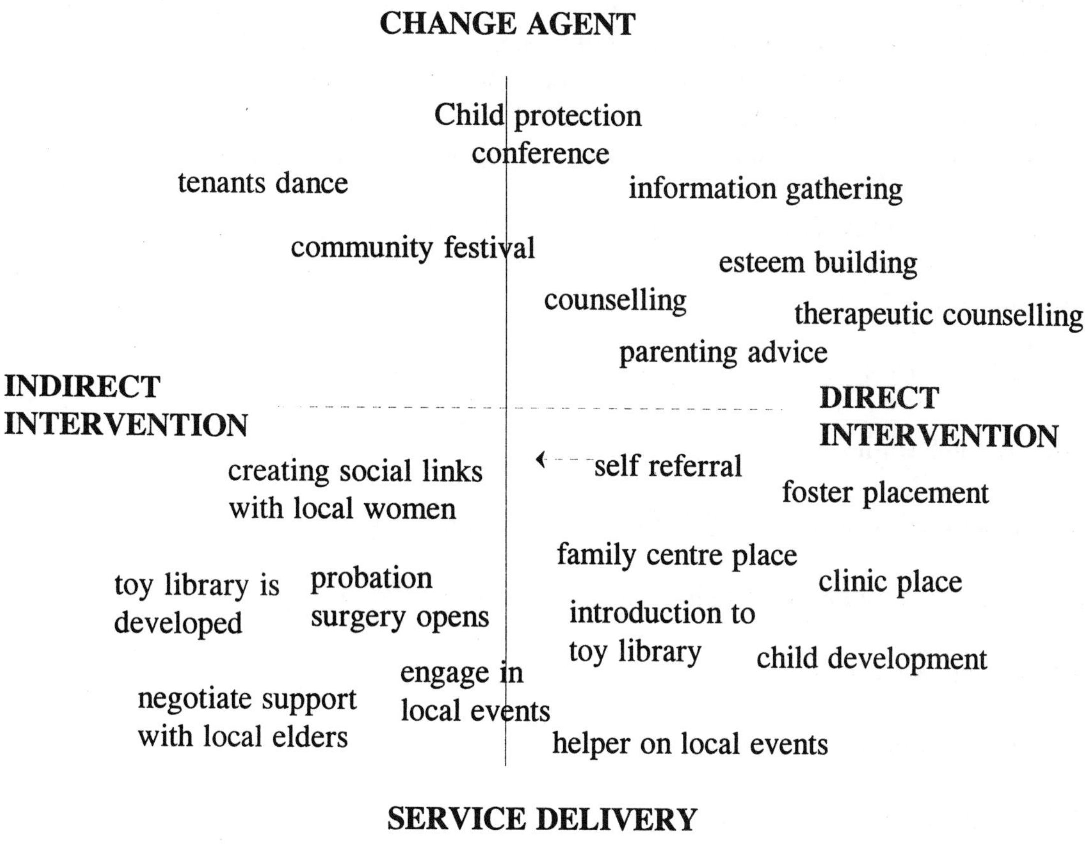

CHANGE AGENT

```
                        Child protection
                          conference
        tenants dance                information gathering
              community festival
                                        esteem building
                              counselling
                                          therapeutic counselling
                              parenting advice

INDIRECT                                        DIRECT
INTERVENTION                                    INTERVENTION
          creating social links    ←- - self referral
          with local women                   foster placement

  toy library is   probation      family centre place
  developed        surgery opens                       clinic place
                                  introduction to
                                  toy library    child development
                            engage in
    negotiate support      local events
    with local elders
                                 helper on local events
```

SERVICE DELIVERY

From: Hearn, B. (1995) *Child and Family Support and Protection: A practical approach.* National Children's Bureau

Appendix 5c

Evaluation of practice development: Brief notes for team managers

Preamble

Managers and practitioners attempting to evaluate the effectiveness of interventions and developments may be daunted by the complexity of the process. Evaluation can take many forms and can indeed be very elaborate and complicated (experimental research) or be a much simpler process (self-evaluation). It can be seen as a way of systematically finding out what is going on/how you are doing, and is essential for improving practice. As well as highlighting the inadequacies, evaluation can help to identify what is being achieved.

One of the first issues to reflect upon is the purpose of the evaluation.

Evaluations can be used to:

- Improve current projects

- Ensure accountability

- Aid rational decisions about continuing or expanding help

- Gain political or economic backing for new projects

- Build budget proposals

- Establish cause-effect relationships.

(Coulshed 1990, p. 169)

Monitoring vs evaluation

It may be helpful at this point to distinguish between monitoring and evaluation.

Monitoring

Monitoring is about collecting information. In social services it is not unusual for a wide variety of information to be collected and presented in lists and charts and seemingly used for no other purpose. Systems are set in place to gather such information over time.

Evaluation

Evaluation is the process of analysing and drawing conclusions from the information collected. It may involve the evaluation of information collected over time, or a particular service or aspect of a service may be evaluated as a one-off. The process put simply is one of posing questions; answering those questions and drawing conclusions from these. It is unlikely however, that any evaluation would progress in a sequential manner. More usually the phases overlap, with answers producing more questions and often the process may have to be gone through repeatedly.

Despite an espoused commitment to evaluation, people are often reluctant to undertake it. Evaluations can be seen as threatening to the reputations of workers, and to the organisation's resources.

Evaluations are complicated by the range of stakeholder interests in any service or organisation. The list of possible stakeholders can seem endless. When planning to evaluate, decisions have to be made about who to include as legitimate stakeholders. Some define stakeholders quite narrowly, confining the list to those with some direct responsibility for making decisions about future practice/projects. Others take a broader view, defining stakeholders as all the people whose lives are affected by the programme and its evaluation. For a service stakeholders will range from the managers, workers, council members or members of management committees, local residents, through to those likely to benefit, ie the direct recipients and possibly their significant others, for example, in the case of a service for children parents/carers are likely stakeholders. Those who are likely to lose out if the project works are also possible stakeholders.

Questions arise about who decides on what to evaluate; how to evaluate; who to involve; what measures to use and the criteria for judging 'good' versus 'poor'. When considering the question 'how well are we doing?', one should always ask 'according to whom?' Negotiating measures of longer term outcomes with a range of stakeholders including users is a difficult issue.

Types of evaluations

There are different types of evaluations. Service evaluations may look at the service as a whole or on different aspects of the service. To determine the effectiveness of particular interventions/projects, requires the simultaneous evaluation of inputs, processes and outcomes.

Inputs: Staff; resources (financial/physical/human); participants.

Process: Focus is on the quality of service delivery. In some circumstances the process may be as important as the outcome. Thus for a child/parent involved in a traumatic investigation, having access to a known/caring/trusted worker throughout can mean a great deal.

When there's a will there's a way

Outcomes: Here the focus is the overall impact of the service/intervention on those at the receiving end. 'Outcome' is not a straightforward concept, and is particularly contentious and difficult when applied to child care. There are different types of outcomes, reflecting different perspectives and interests. Parker and others identify five:

      i)   public outcomes;
      ii)   service outcomes;
      iii)   professional outcomes;
      iv)   family outcomes;
      v)   child outcomes.

(Parker and others (1991) *Looking after Children: Assessing Outcomes in Child Care*)

A reduction of the number of children looked after may be seen as a positive service outcome, but may be of little interest or meaning to the individual child/family or indeed the public.

A further issue to consider is the extent to which the focus should be the 'group' or the 'individual'.

In discussing the development of performance measures relevant to outcomes in child care, Knapp (1989) points out that:

'Little is known about the impacts of child care interventions in child, family and social welfare, still less about how best to measure them and a plurality of methodologies is needed' (Knapp 1989, *Measuring Child Care Outcomes* p.27).

Knapp developed a 'production of welfare' framework:

- Resource/inputs: staff, physical, capital, provisions and other consumables;

- Non-resource inputs: personalities, activities and attitudes of staff;

- Intermediate outcomes: measures of quality of care rather than quality of life;

- Final outcomes: changes in child welfare, defined in terms of society's objectives for child care and child development (self-esteem, mental health, social networks, peer relationships, interpersonal skills);

- Throughputs and processes: child care practices.

Approaches to evaluation

The following are some approaches used in social research. The important point about these approaches, is that they have different rationales and will be more or less appropriate depending on the particular circumstances. There are those for whom the experimental design carries the most kudos but given the nature of social work it is extremely limited. Although the approaches are set out as distinct and separate, they are not mutually exclusive, often when a service is being evaluated, different approaches have to be used simultaneously to examine different aspects.

The following approaches to evaluation were identified in the Open University course 'Managing voluntary and non-profit organisations', in the module on 'Evaluation and effectiveness'.

1. Experimental research

Least likely to be of relevance to the needs of practising managers. It is highly technical, prolonged and time-consuming and expensive.

2. Quasi-experimental evaluation

Includes for example, many 'before and after' studies. May be more relevant to practising managers but still demands that questions are narrowly focused and can still be time-consuming.

3. Performance assessment and measures

Evaluation in public sector management has largely focused on mechanisms for performance measurement, with the four e's - economy, efficiency, effectiveness and equity - providing a framework for evaluating organisational performance. Some examples of indicators include:

Economy - costs.
Efficiency - productivity.
Effectiveness - client satisfaction and changes in client welfare.
Equity - staff profiles.

Performance assessment is about determining whether the objectives of a service are met and the values accorded with, and these must therefore be explicit.

4. Pluralistic evaluation

Pluralistic evaluation recognises the range and differing perspectives of stakeholders. As this approach has to take into account this diversity of views it can be of help in negotiating agreement on priorities.

5. *Illuminative evaluation*

Involves people 'taking stock' and sharing their understanding of the situation. It is not about goal achievement but more usually looking at working practices which may only have an indirect impact on goals, or re-examining assumptions about needs and priorities as new information/demands come to light.

Types of measures: quantitative or qualitative

There is a long-running tension in social research about quantitative vs qualitative measures, and a tendency to debate the validity of one over the other.

In social work, a combination of the two is usually necessary to make any sense of the impact of interventions.

Talking about measures can encourage an emphasis on the quantitative, by focusing on crude numbers as measures of success. These measures might include: numbers referred, numbers on child protection registers, number of children looked after and caseload figures. A danger in this focus on crude figures, is that they can then be used to determine resource allocation. Numbers by themselves do not tell us much about what is actually happening in practice. They should be treated as 'triggers' for analysis.

Qualitative measures tend to focus on the meaning of the intervention from the participants' perspective.

Tips and cautions

- Team managers are most likely to be concerned with evaluating the team's work and are less likely to be concerned with large-scale evaluation exercises.

- Be able to answer the question 'Why are you evaluating?'. This will help to determine what you measure and how. For example if the team's aim is to encourage greater user involvement and working in partnership then it would be very important to look at processes and procedures.

- Who is interested in the outcome of your evaluation? Whose interest should take priority?

- Be selective about what you measure. You won't be able to measure everything.

- Quantitative and qualitative measures are not mutually exclusive. For example you could monitor the changes in the numbers of children attending child protection conferences, while getting qualitative information on how they experience it, benefit from it and the nature of their involvement in the process.

- Decide what outcome measures are most appropriate; whose outcomes are most important and who should have a say in the decision. Should the focus be on long term or short term outcomes?

- What will you be comparing your information with? Last year? Before and after? Another service?

- Evaluation should not be an end in itself. The findings are supposed to help improve practice and if they are not implemented then managers should question the purpose of the evaluation.

- Try to create a culture which encourages evaluation in all aspects of the team's work, from supervision, through to casework, group work and other specific projects.

- Teams are likely to be involved in practice developments/initiatives which will go through a phase (sometimes lengthy) of preparing the ground; building up contacts and relationships; raising awareness and resources and obtaining resources and training. To keep on track it is important that measures appropriate to this phase of the process are devised. For example is the team devoting more time to practice discussions as opposed to business? How many and what range of agencies have been consulted in the process? How many children and families have been consulted with? Is there a report which brings together feedback from the consultation as an output from this phase?

- How will you pick up the unexpected and the overlooked or the negatives? One of the dangers of focusing too narrowly on pre-determined targets and outcomes is that you will miss important information along the way.

- In planning the evaluation, remember that although there are wide differences, all approaches take time and have some cost implications. Allow for this.

Some quantitative information which you may wish to monitor

- Children on the child protection register.
- Self-referrals vs professional referrals.
- Referrals to local voluntary projects such as Home Start and Newpin.
- Child protection investigations undertaken.
- Cases allocated where children are not on child protection register/'looked after'.
- Children 'looked after' (court orders vs accommodated).
- Ethnic breakdown of those receiving support services/child protection register/care orders/accommodated.
- Children attending child protection conferences.
- Percentage of respondents in the user survey expressing satisfaction/dissatisfaction with the service.

This information would then have to be analysed to determine the relevance and importance.

Other measures of progress

- A joint agenda with the local community for an initiative/development which reflects local needs.

- If an objective is to develop services appropriate to minority ethnic groups, then are such developments in progress?

- If promoting the involvement of children and/or parents in the process, is there a report written by them or which they have signed up to as reflecting their views?

Appendix 6

User survey

Section one: the office: Address

a) Why did you come to our office?

b) How did you find out about our office? (for example, did a friend or neighbour tell you about us?)

c) If you heard about us from someone else, what did they tell you about the kind of work done here and the kind of reasons people come to see us?

d) When you need help or advice who would you usually go to? (Tick the most appropriate)

> Relative
> Partner
> Friends
> Neighbours
> Local policeman
> Local councillors
> Citizen's Advice Bureau
> Health visitor
> Teacher
> Doctor
> Others (please state)

e) Was it easy to find our office the first time you came?

This page may be photocopied for use within your organisation. © National Children's Bureau

When there's a will there's a way

f)   What happened when you arrived on this visit - did you have a long time to wait, for example?

g)   What did you first think about our office? Did you feel it was a warm and friendly place, or did it seem official and unpleasant?

h)   Did you change your mind later on? If so why?

i)   When did you first make a call to this office?

Section two: the people (on this visit)

a)   Who did you see?

b)   Did you have any choice?

c)   Would you have liked to choose who you saw?

d)   Did the person you saw tell you his/her name?

e)   Would you have liked to know his/her name?

When there's a will there's a way

f) Was the person you saw: (please tell us about the words which don't apply and other words if you want to)
    Helpful
    Sympathetic
    Caring
    Unpleasant
    Off-hand
    Understanding
    Other (please state)

g) Did you feel you could talk to with the person you saw about many different things?

h) Did you think the worker was: (please tick)

- someone to give you advice?
- someone to be friendly with you?
- someone to listen to you?
- someone to do something on your behalf?
- someone to sort out a problem?

Section three: the problem

a) Did you come to our office for advice, or did you feel you wanted something more?

b) Did you think of going anywhere else for help?

c) Was this office your first or last choice?

This page may be photocopied for use within your organisation. © National Children's Bureau

When there's a will there's a way

d) Do you think that you learnt enough to be able to solve a similar problem yourself next time?

Section four: the service

a) What service/help/advice did you expect when you first came to the office?

b) Did you get what you expected?

c) Were you satisfied with how the worker dealt with your query?

d) What did the worker do?

e) Did the worker make clear what he/she would do for you?

f) Did he/she involve you in making decisions?

g) Do you think the worker understood your problem?

Finally

- If a friend or relation had a similar sort of problem to you, would you recommend him/her to visit this office?

- Is there anything I haven't asked which you think you would like to tell us?

- Is there anything you would like to ask us?

This page may be photocopied for use within your organisation. © National Children's Bureau

Appendix 7a

Child protection and child welfare
Messages from Research: translation into practice

When to use: Team discussion/training session/team day following presentation or reading of overview from recent child protection research

Exercise 1: response to research findings (45 mins)

In small groups (no more than six per group is advisable) discuss your response to the research findings and conclusions, focusing in particular on the following:

a) What, for you, are the most surprising findings?

b) Which findings/conclusions fit with your experience of practice locally?

c) Which are most confirming of the values which underpin your own practice, and are generally supportive of your approach?

d) Which messages present the greatest challenge to you as practitioners/ managers? Why?

Each small group should summarise its responses to **(b)** and **(d)** to all participants in a large group.

Preparation for manager: Read *Child Protection: Messages from Research*. Handout in advance to all participant, copies of Davies C, & Little M (1995) 'Family Circle' *Community Care* 22 June 1995.

Materials: Pens, flip-chart.

Appendix 7b

Child protection and child welfare
Messages from Research: translation into practice

Purpose: This is an awareness-raising exercise to enable practitioners to consider the potential impact on practice by working on case material provided. It is about exploring and debating options, not about prescribing a correct way.

When to use: You will need a one-page summary of a case of a child in need with some protection issues. Use the exercise for team/area/inter-agency awareness raising session. Have available the department's child protection guidelines, a copy of *Working Together* and a copy of a guide to the Children Act (1989) for reference. It is likely to highlight different interpretations of local child protection guidelines and possible gaps in knowledge, for example of the provisions in Section 17 of the Children Act (1989). Other agencies/departmental or Department of Health guidelines are likely to be put forward as the reasons for stronger interventions. Team managers will have to tease out what is informing practice and the extent to which it is being driven by fear and anxiety. Managers will need to highlight good practice and encourage shared ownership and responsibility for decision-making. This exercise is likely to highlight areas for further work with the team, for example on approaches to assessment.

Exercise 2: Case study exercise (1 hour)

Part I (20 mins)

In your groups read through the material provided and discuss:

a) What would be the most likely response to this case? How would it be categorised?

b) What scope is there within local procedures and expectations for professionals to exercise discretion when deciding what action to take?

c) What degree of consensus is there within the group on these points? How would you explain this?

Appendix 7b

Child protection and child welfare
Messages from Research: translation into practice

Exercise 2: Case study exercise

Part II (40 mins)

The research highlights concerns about the narrow focus on abusive incidents; the emphasis on 'investigations', rather than 'making enquiries'; interventions driven by concerns with safety, but rarely addressing wider welfare needs.

Consider the following list of possible responses to the case and discuss the points raised below.

Some possible responses

- Social work visit to the child and family to assess possible need for services, leaving open the question of a Section 47 enquiry until after this initial assessment.

- Social services check information held by police and other agencies, then initiate Section 17 assessment. The care management plan is developed, monitored and reviewed through a series of planning meetings.

- Discussion with the police but social services alone carrying out Section 47 'enquiry'. Range of possible outcomes, for example, provision of family support services; further investigation; assessment.

- Professionals' meeting to decide on level of response.

- Strategy discussion/meeting, followed by Section 47 investigation carried out jointly by police and social services.

Points for discussion

- The potential consequences, both positive or negative of each response.

- Why did you decide which approach would be most appropriate to the needs of the child(ren) and family. What informed your decision?

When there's a will there's a way

- The next step. Who would you need to involve? How will you explain your response to the referrer/other agencies? How will you approach the family and how will you explain the work you are proposing to do?

Feedback to large group on the response you decided was most appropriate and the factors which informed your decision.

Appendix 7c

Exercise on partnership and participation

Time 1.5 hours

Partnership with parents has been shown to be vital in child protection work if children's needs are to be met and better outcomes achieved. Researchers found that workers recognised the value of partnership but were some way off achieving this in practice.

This exercise is adapted from Exercise 9 in *Messages from Research* and Exercise 12 in *The Challenge of Partnership in Child Protection* (Department of Health. Social Services Inspectorate, 1994). It can be used in development work with team leaders or team leaders can adapt if for use with their teams.

Aim of the exercise: To explore what is meant by partnership and participation and to enable professionals to evaluate the extent to which this is a feature of practice within their agencies.

Preliminary task: Read the summary of the research by Thoburn, Shemmings and Lewis 'Paternalism or Partnership? Family Involvement in the Child Protection Process' in Bullock, R (1995) *Child Protection: Messages from Research*. HMSO

1. Consider each of the features in the following **Partnership List** (from *The Challenge of Partnership in Child Protection*) and decide the relevance to work with parents in your agency in all areas of practice, not just meetings.

Partnership list (professional to parents)	Relevant	Not relevant	Not sure
Shared values			
A shared task or goal			
Both (or all) parties contribute resources and/or skills			
Trust between the partners			
Negotiation of plans			
Decisions made together			
Mutual confidence that each partner can and will 'deliver'			
Equality or near equality between parties			
Choice in entering partnership			

When there's a will there's a way

Partnership list (professional to parents)	Relevant	Not relevant	Not sure
Formalised framework of agreed working arrangements			
Open sharing of information			
Mechanisms for monitoring, reviewing and ending of partnership			
Dealing with power issues			

2. On a scale of one to five - 1 = good, 5 = poor

   Rate the performance of:
   a) your agency
   b) your team
   c) yourself

   Partnership with families during:
   i) investigations/enquiries phase prior to conference;
   ii) assessment phase;
   iii) support and treatment phase.

   Place your chosen number in the relevant box

	Your team	Yourself	Your agency
Investigation			
Assessment			
Support & treat			

3. What is the purpose of family members attending child protection case conferences?

4. What factors might make it difficult for families to attend conferences?

5. What does your agency offer parents/families to overcome these and any other difficulties? How can matters be improved?

6. How does your agency seek and take account of family members' views of the conference process, and of their views of the degree of partnership?

7. How can you, as a manager, ensure that staff share their learning about the practice of partnership? How can lessons be consolidated into better practice?

8. Learning from experience requires a climate in which problems experienced in practice are seen as opportunities for learning not as uncomfortable failures. How do you ensure that this is happening?

9. Consider the tips for practice and policy highlighted by Thoburn and others:

   a) to what extent do these reflect the current situation in your agency?

   b) what would you like to improve or develop?

   c) identify three steps you intend to take within the next six weeks towards this end.

Appendix 7d

Questions for individual team managers

Based on material from Farmer and Owen (1995)
Child Protection Practice: Private risks and public remedies

Purpose

To enable team managers/practitioners to reflect on and begin to address the questions of effectiveness in child protection practice.

When/how to use: Designed for use with/by team managers. Can be adapted for use with practitioners by looking at workloads for example. The exercise can be done in full/in part and be used as part of supervision/development activity. It could inform team planning.

Part I - 45 minutes

Farmer and Owen identified the following aims for the child protection system:

- protection of children from harm;

- promotion of children's physical, emotional and intellectual development (for example, welfare); and

- meeting the needs of other family members.

---

1. Do you agree that the above are the key aims of the child protection system?
   Do you view them as being of equal importance?
   If not, how do you prioritise them?

2. Would you know the extent to which all or any of the above aims were being achieved in your team?
   Are all aims being achieved to the same level?
   How would you explain differences, if there are any, in the levels of achievement?

3. What systems/methods have you set up to enable you to monitor outcomes?

4. Would the workers in your team agree with your assessment of performance in relation to the above aims?
   What would their views be?

When there's a will there's a way

5. What do parents/children say about the team's effectiveness in relation to these aims?

Part II - 45 minutes

> **At the 20 month follow-up period Farmer and Owen found that:**
>
> - 70 per cent had been protected;
> - 68 per cent welfare enhanced; and
> - 30 per cent of primary carer/parent needs met.

1. How would you rate the above performance on a scale of 0-10, where 10 = excellent and 0 = unacceptable?

2. How do these figures compare to your own team's performance?

3. What are you most satisfied with and least satisfied with?

4. What plans/strategies have you put in place to improve performance?

5. What are the likely blocks and how do you plan to deal with them?

6. What factors are likely to enable you to bring about the desired changes?

Part III - 45 minutes

> **Some reasons for the deficits in children's welfare were due to:**
>
> a) unsatisfactory placements in care;
>
> b) no direct services offered/maintained because concerns quickly diminished after registration.

1. Does the practice b) apply in your team?

2. If no, how do you know that it doesn't?
   If yes, do you think it should/could be changed, and why?

3. If change is desirable and possible, what ideas have you got about how to begin to move in the desired direction?

4. What would you need in order to implement your ideas?

Part IV - 30 minutes

> **Farmer and Owen identified that:**
>
> a) the needs of the primary carer were met through planned, purposeful social work, by practitioners who strove to understand and address a range of parental needs; and
>
> b) it is common for needs of main care giver to be given little priority in child protection work.

1. Which of the above statements are closer to the practice in your team?
   How do you know?

2. Would parents agree?
   How do you know what their views would be?

3. Do you see b) as inevitable/understandable?
   Why do you say that?

4. Can parents' and children's needs be totally separated and if so, when?
   What are some of the likely consequences of this approach?

Appendix 7e

Exercise for team leaders: Identifying elements of good practice within their teams

When/how to use: Designed to be used with/by team managers working individually or with their peers in small groups. The questions are designed to get a sense of a team manager's impressions of his/her team as a whole, and to give pointers for areas of further work/action. It can be adapted for use with individual practitioners.

Time: 1 hour

The summary of DH-commissioned research into child protection systems, *Child Protection: Messages from Research* (pages 45-52) sets out five pre-conditions for effective practice which had been identified by all the studies.

The key pre-conditions are:

- sensitive and informed professional practice;
- an appropriate balance of power between participants;
- a wider perspective on child protection;
- effective supervision and training of social workers;
- services which enhance children's general quality of life.

1. How satisfied are you with your practitioners' performance in these areas?

    Are you: very satisfied/satisfied/dissatisfied/very dissatisfied?

2. Would practitioners agree with your assessment?

3. How do you know that practitioners are performing to such standards?

4. What have you done to ensure that such practice standards are adopted or maintained?

5. What is your understanding of having a 'wider perspective'?

This page may be photocopied for use within your organisation. © National Children's Bureau

When there's a will there's a way

6. Do your colleagues and your team share this understanding?

7. If your answer to either or both questions 5 and 6 is 'don't know', what could you do to address this?

8. Would you say that the team ethos necessary for expanding the use of family support services is present in your team? If yes, specify the key elements. If no, what are you going to do to help create such an ethos?

Appendix 7f

Exercise: The child protection process: criteria for decision making

(Adapted from Exercise 4 in *Child Protection: Messages from Research*. To be used with small groups of team leaders and/or practitioners in a 2-3 hour session)

Out of approximately 160,000 child protection referrals made annually to social services departments, research estimates that only 40,000 are conferenced and fewer than 25,000 lead to a name being placed on the child protection register. (Bullock 1995, p.105).

This exercise seeks to establish the criteria used in your authority to process cases through the system. It will increase understanding about the different reasons professionals have for referring children to the protection services and their differing expectations of what it can achieve.

Preliminary tasks

- Be familiar with the diagram on page 28 of *Child Protection: Messages from Research* (Bullock 1995) and the summary of study done by Gibbons, Conroy and Bell given on pages 68-70 and pages 33-34.
- Bring a copy of your agency's child protection procedures to the session.

Select four recently referred cases, from across the team/area, collaborating with your colleagues beforehand, using the following criteria:

- one which was referred but not investigated;
- one which was investigated but there was a decision not to conference;
- one conferenced but where a child was not registered; and
- one conferenced and where a child was registered.

1. **Examine each case to decide the following**

- What criteria were used to reach the decision?
- What family needs were established in the enquiry?
- What support services, if any, were offered to the family?

2. **Consider your findings in the light of your agency's procedures**

- Compare them with the research findings concerning factors that determined which cases proceeded through different stages of the child protection system (summary of pages 33-34).
- Look again at the factors that apply in your area. What does a comparison indicate about your local system?

3. **Review the exercise and try to answer the following questions**

- Was it easy to establish the criteria being used?
- Do your present procedures provide clear criteria for reaching decisions at each stage?
- Did the decision-making process focus on the abusive activity or on the broader needs of the family?
- At what stage in the process were the families' needs defined?
- Could the families' needs have been defined and services offered at an earlier stage?
- Would these services have changed the extent to which the cases were involved in the child protection system?

4. **Learning from the exercise**

- Note the key things you have learnt about the criteria you use in making decisions.

- What are the similarities and the differences between yourself and others in the group?

- How do your procedures help or hinder the process?

- Specify two changes you would like to see to the procedures.

- Identify two things that you will do within the next month to ensure that families' needs are defined and services offered to meet those needs, at an earlier stage in the process.

Appendix 7g

What happens in your local child protection system?

For any experienced professional. This exercise could take place as a team development activity over a number of weeks. Information could then be created as a team resource subsequently to be maintained and updated.

It emerged from the research that approximately 160,000 children and families a year are drawn into the child protection process but that the names of fewer than 25,000 children are registered. It appeared that many of the children and families would benefit from services under Section 17 of the Children Act 1989 and that providing services by those means would increase parental cooperation, one of the key indicators of successful intervention.

Aim To encourage the use of research and monitoring information to inform and improve local policy and practice.

Preliminary tasks

Be familiar with page 28 in the Overview and summaries of the research by Gibbons, Conroy and Bell on pp.68-70.

1. Ask participants if they know what type of statistical information about child protection is collected locally and nationally. Divide into pairs or small groups and set each the task of collecting information to answer one or more of the following questions:

- How many referrals are received by your agency team each year?
- How many child abuse investigations take place each year?
- How many investigations lead to a child being removed from home?
- How many lead to Emergency Protection Orders?
- How many cases result in a child protection conference being called?
- How many lead to court proceedings?
- In how many cases was the perpetrator removed from the home?
- In how many cases were further services offered following investigation?

2. In the light of this evidence, it is important to consider whether a particular authority has a high or low conferencing and registration rate. Therefore an attempt should be made to compare results with other authorities of similar population size and characteristics. Staff in high registering authorities need to ask themselves:

(You will need to refer to the Department of Health publication *Children and Young People on Child Protection Registers* prepared annually by the Government Statistical Office.)

- How many criteria on page 31 of the Overview apply to your authority?
- Should any action be taken to alter this?

When there's a will there's a way

Staff in low registering authorities need to ask themselves:

- What percentages of cases not registered are closed without further action?
- What percentage of cases which are not registered go on to be considered in a multi-agency forum to decide whether the children are in need? How many subsequently receive a service and from which agency?
- What percentage of cases investigated but not conferenced are considered in a multi-agency forum?
- How many go on to receive a service and from which agency?
- What percentage of cases conferenced but not registered receive services and from which agencies?

From: Bullock, R and others (1995) *Child Protection: Messages from Research*. HMSO

Appendix 7h

The relationship between need, protection and welfare.

For team leaders meeting as a group or team leaders and their staff.

The research shows that agencies involved in child protection are often too remote from family support services, each having their own staff, ways of working and resources. Since the problems faced by children and families are complex, practical benefits can come from an approach which merges questions about the child's protection with others about support for the family.

Aim   To clarity the relationship between need, protection and welfare by closely examining cases.

Preliminary tasks

Be familiar with pp.53-56 in the Overview. It may be helpful for the group undertaking the task to split into pairs to look at the cases and to regroup to discuss findings.

Data collection

Choose four cases currently being offered family support services via a family centre or other support facilities, such as day care, homestart, etc.

1. Examine each case in detail and decide:

- Who sought the services and for what reasons?
- What criteria were used to decide whether the family should be offered a service?
- What family needs were established?
- What was the intended outcome of the package of support being offered?
- Are there child protection issues in these families?

Data collection

Choose four cases currently the subject of a child protection plan.
Repeat the process described in Step One and compare the results with your analysis of the family support service cases.

2. Look a the two sets of answers and consider:

- What are the similarities within the two groups, those offered family support services and those the subject of a child protection plan, in terms of the needs established and services offered?
- How do the criteria differ?
- How do the established needs differ?

When there's a will there's a way

- How do the services provided differ?

Do you think that a continuum of services as described on page 56 would provide a better framework for these cases?

From: Bullock, R and others (1995) *Child Protection: Messages from Research*. HMSO

Appendix 7i

Exercise: Definition and development of family support

Purpose: For teams/practitioners working together to examine and reach agreement and improve understanding of family support.

Time: 1.5 - 2 hours for full examination of all questions.

1. Consider the following statements: How do they relate to your own experience?

    - Recent research points to the need for reframing child protection - currently too *'system-centred'* rather than *'child-centred'*. (Hearn 1995, p.9)

    - Current practice has made child protection the gateway to support services. We urgently need integrated understanding of work which both protects children and supports families in need.

    - Work has become focused around abusive events without attention to context.

    - There is a need for *'more emphasis on understanding and working with relationships which surround event(s), most importantly building on positive dimensions which already exist'*. (Hearn 1995)

2. *'Effective support and assistance means protection but protection activity alone may not mean effective support and assistance'*. (Hearn 1995, p.15)

    - Discuss this statement with others in your group. Is there a shared understanding of what this means in practice?

This page may be photocopied for use within your organisation. © National Children's Bureau

When there's a will there's a way

3. Consider these two definitions of family support:

The Audit Commission

'Family support is an activity or facility aimed at providing advice and support to parents to help them in bringing up their children'. The Audit Commission (1994): *Seen but not Heard*

Alternative definition

'Family support is about the creation and enhancement, with and for families in need, of locally based (or accessible) facilities, activities and networks, the use of which will have outcomes such as alleviated stress, increased self esteem, promoted parental/carer/family competence and behaviour and increased parental/carer capacity to nurture and protect children' Hearn, B (1995) *Child and family support and protection: A practical approach.*

How useful do you find these definitions? Discuss in your group and come up with a definition which is most helpful to you.

4.
- Do you have a supportive political and policy context for developing family support?

- Do you know whether an audit of services provided has been done? Do you or your team have a comprehensive list of local family support services?

- Does your agency or team have a strategy for addressing the identified gaps? If not, how could you begin to influence developments?

Appendix 7j

Exercise for team managers
Conceptual framework for family support work

Purpose: Gives a framework for team managers to begin to get an overview of current work and from there develop more detailed systems for auditing.

How to use: Team managers will have to do work on this in their work place, within an agreed period.

A useful way of conceptualising family support work might be to look at the theoretical framework devised by Hardiker and others (1991). She looks at the questions 'what is being prevented?', 'how?' and 'for whom?', and identifies different levels of intervention.

Utting, D (1995) Family and Parenthood. Rowntree Foundation	
Primary:	Universally available services which are expected to strengthen family functioning.
Secondary:	Support services targeted on families in early difficulties where the risks of breakdown are, as yet, low.
Tertiary:	Work with families who are suffering severe and well-established difficulties.
Fourth dimension:	Concerned with post-crisis work. Aim could be seen as damage limitation. Efforts directed at minimising lasting adverse effects during and following separation from parents and at providing support to parents and to children who are being looked after.

Exercise: issues to consider

- How would your current team **work load** fit into the above categories?

- Would your current information systems allow you to audit work done on duty and assign to above categories?

- If yes, answer the first question for work done on duty.

- If no, begin to think about what information you would need to collect in order to be able to answer such a question and how you might go about setting up a system for collecting such information?

This page may be photocopied for use within your organisation. © National Children's Bureau

Appendix 7k

Exercise for practitioners/managers
Community support for families

Purpose: Practitioners to pool views and information on community supports. Useful starting point for team wanting to:

    a) create resources map/file;
    b) improve relationships with communities;
    c) wanting to map needs/resources.

Time: 1 - 1.5 hours

i) Together reflect on the role of the community(ies) in supporting children and families.

ii) Exchange information on examples of community support activities that you are aware of in your area; Who initiated them? Who runs them currently? From where do they get support? What role do professionals have in them? What are some of the benefits to children and families of this form of support? Are there issues of access for some families and how could these be overcome?

iii) How do you currently work with the community(ies) in your area? What are some of the potential benefits to you of working with community networks?

iv) What could you do to work more effectively with communities towards enhancing children's general quality of life?

This page may be photocopied for use within your organisation. © National Children's Bureau

Appendix 7l

Exercise for team leaders and their staff teams

Defining, prioritising and measuring extent of needs

Purpose: For practitioners to begin to consider definitions and mapping of needs and to develop local plans/services to address such needs.

When/how to use: Over a number of team practice sessions held at six week intervals; incorporate a presentation summarising key issues.

Allow two hours for Part II and similar for Part III.

Part I: For team leaders working on their own or with other team leaders

Preliminary tasks

- Read **Children's Services Planning: Guidance** (HMSO 1996)
- Read the summary of the Audit Commission report, *Seen but not Heard*.
- Familiarise yourself with authority's children's services plan.
- Have available any local procedures or guidance regarding children in need.
- Be familiar with Section 17 of the Children Act.

Consider the following:

1. How has your authority responded to the (now mandatory) requirement to draw up children's services plans? How easy was it to get hold of a) the plan and b) the DH guidance on drawing up plans.

2. How is 'need' defined in your authority?
   Does this concur with your understanding of the concept?

3. Is there a jointly agreed definition with the health authority?

4. How are these needs then prioritised?
   Do you agree with these priorities and how strictly do you apply them in your work?

5. What tools/mechanisms/systems are used for measuring the extent of needs in your authority?

6. What happens about measuring needs within your locality?
   Where does the information come from and who is involved in the process?

Part II: For team leaders to do with their teams in a planning session

Preliminary task

Workers should be supplied with relevant material and should read these before the workshop.

1. Practitioners to do Part I in pairs.

2. In the whole group discuss what information is and isn't known. How could this information be obtained?

3. In relation to question 5 in Part I, pool ideas about what workers think:
   - happens currently;
   - should happen, for example, what other means could be used and which key local professionals or organisations are likely to have relevant information;
   - devise an action plan which would enable the team to get a better understanding of local needs and if/how they are currently being met;
   - needs which are not being met.

4. Assign tasks and set time-scale (for example, six weeks) for reviewing progress.

Part III: For team leaders and their teams as follow up to Parts I & II

Having gathered information about local needs and resources:

1. Prioritise needs; determine the extent to which they are already catered for.

2. Identify other needs which should or could be met.

3. How could the team begin to address such needs?

4. Devise a strategy to address 2 and 3.

5. Consider:
   - Who are the potential partners in any development?
   - If there is a clearly identified project/scheme that is needed, how might you begin to develop it?

When there's a will there's a way

- Discuss what the involvement of your team could and should be, for example:

    o   lead role in development;
    o   run project;
    o   ongoing support role;
    o   funding;
    o   link person and so on.

- Develop an action plan for this development with tasks and time-scales for review and completion.

Appendix 7m

Reviewing input and evaluating outcomes

Purpose: For practitioners and managers to consider their approach to evaluation. For use as part of a particular session on evaluation **or** incorporated into a training event.

Time: 1 hour

a) How often do you review the work you do with children and families? What dictates the frequency of these work reviews? Who do you involve in the review?

b) How do you assess whether/not what you are doing is making a positive difference to the lives of children and families?

c) When evaluating outcomes, do you canvas the views of the children you are working with: i) as a matter of course?
 ii) in some circumstances?

What influences whether or not children's views are sought?

d) Do you seek the views of parents and other family members?

e) What outcome measures do you tend to focus on?

f) How are the views of children and families incorporated into practice and service development within the team and wider department?

g) What other methods could you and your colleagues use to improve upon this aspect of practice?

This page may be photocopied for use within your organisation. © National Children's Bureau

Appendix 7n

Walking the scale
Steps towards refocused practice

Exercise for team sessions

Useful for a) Warm-up (20 mins)   b) Goal-setting (45 mins)

1.
   - Get into pairs. Person A and B lay out a scale from 1 to 10 on the floor by using small pieces of paper. '1' stands for polarised practice ie. child protection versus family support, with an over-reliance on procedures and '10' stands for competent integrated practice, with family support as the context for child protection work with procedures providing a framework and are being used flexibly to guide decisions.

   - B asks A to step into the position on the scale and to tell him/her about what he/she is doing at that point. Talk about the skills, knowledge and values which led A to step into that position.

2.
   - B asks A to go to the next step on the scale. The question now is 'What are you doing at this position? What's different here? What will you need to do to get here? Who and what can help you?

3.
   - A and B change roles and repeat the exercices.

Letter to yourself

4.
   - Now A and B start to write a letter to themselves answering the following question:

     'What will I do in the next three months to maintain and to improve my position on the scale? How will I know it?'.

5.
   - Write your address on the envelope and give the letter to your partner. Ask him/her to send it back to you in three months time.

Adapted from European Brief Therapy Conference, London 1995

Bibliography

Audit Commission (1994a) *Seen but Not Heard: Co-ordinating Community Child Health and Social Services for Children in Need. Detailed Evidence and Guidelines for Managers and Practitioners.* HMSO

Audit Commission (1994b) *Seen but Not Heard: Co-ordinating Community Child Health and Social Services for Children in Need. Executive Summary.* HMSO

Bebbington, A, and Miles, J (1989) 'The background of children who enter local authority care', *British Journal of Social Work*, 19, 5, pp.349-368

Berridge, D, and Cleaver, H (1987) *Foster Home Breakdown.* Blackwell

Bullock, R, and others (1995) *Child Protection: Messages from Research.* HMSO. (Studies in Child Protection).

Bullock, R, Little, M, and Millham, S (1993) *Going Home: the return of children separated from their families.* Dartmouth

Burton, S (unpublished) *Research Summaries on Child Protection and Family Support.* National Children's Bureau

Coulshed, V (1990) *Management in social work.* BASW/Macmillan

Crosbie, D and Vickery, A (1989) *Community Based Schemes in Area Offices.* National Institute for Social Work.

Davies, C and Little, M (1995) 'Family circle', *Community Care*, no.1073 (22 Jun) pp.18-19

Department of Health. Social Services Inspectorate (1994) *The Challenge of Partnership in Child Protection: a practice guide.* HMSO

Department of Health, and Welsh Office (1994) *Children Act Report 1993.* HMSO

Department of Health, and Welsh Office (1995) *Children Act Report 1994.* HMSO

Department of Health (1991) *Patterns and Outcomes in Child Placement: Messages from Current Research and their Implications.* HMSO

Edwards, C (1995) 'Are children better off following protective interventions ?', *Child and Family Law Quarterly*, vol.7. no.3 (Sep). pp.136-151

Farmer, E, and Owen, M (1995) *Child Protection Practice: Private Risks and Public Remedies.* HMSO

Fisher, T (1995) *A Systematic Knowledge Base in Child Protection: What Knowledge do Social Workers Use?* York University

Garnett, L (1992) *Leaving Care and After*. National Children's Bureau

Gibbons, J, and Thorpe, S (1989) 'Can voluntary support projects help vulnerable families? The work of Home-Start', *British Journal of Social Work*, 19, 3, pp.189-202

Gibbons, J, Conroy, S, and Bell, C (1995) *Operating the Child Protection System: A Study of Child Protection Practices in English Local Authorities*. HMSO. (Studies in Child Protection).

Gill, O (1995) 'Neighbourhood watch', *Community Care*, No.1071, 8 Jun, pp.30-31

Hardiker, P, Exton, K, and Barker, M (1991) *Policies and Practices in Preventive Child Care*. Avebury

Hearn, B (1995) *Child and Family Support and Protection: A Practical Approach*. National Children's Bureau

Hearn, B, Darvill, G, and Morris, B (1992) *On Becoming a Manager in Social Work*. Longman.

Hirst, J (1996) 'Family planning', *Community Care*, no.1119, 9 May, pp.16-17.

Jones, S, and Joss, R 'Models of professionalism' *in* Yelloly, M and Henkl, ed. (1995) *Learning and Teaching in Social Work*. Jessica Kingsley.

Knapp, M (1987) *Child Care Outcomes: the Basic Principles Underlying Practical Measurement*, Discussion Paper 557. Personal Social Services Research Unit, University of Kent at Canterbury

Linehan, T (1996) 'The family way', *Community Care*, No.1108, 22 Feb, p.10

Little, M, and Taylor, K (1995) 'Balance of power'. *Community Care* (supplement), No.1079, 27 Jul, p.2-3

Mercer, C (1995) 'A winning prescription', *Community Care*, No.1089, 5 Oct, p.24

Morris, K, and Tunnard, J (eds) (1996) *Family Group Conferences: Messages from UK Practice and Research*. Family Rights Group.

Morrison, T (1993) *Staff Supervision in Social Care: An Action Learning Approach*. Longman.

NCH Action for Children (1996) *Children Still in Need: Refocusing Child Protection in the Context of Children in Need.* NCH Action for Children.

Platt, D, and Shemmings, D (1996) *Making Enquiries into Alleged Child Abuse and Neglect: Partnership with Families.* Pennant Professional Books.

Schon, D A (1983) *The Reflective Practitioner: How Professionals Think in Action.* Temple Smith

Schon, D A (1987) *Educating the Reflective Practitioner.* San Francisco: Jossey-Bass.

Smale, G G (1996) *Mapping Change and Innovation.* HMSO

Stein, M, and Carey, K (1986) *Leaving Care.* Blackwell

Utting, D (1995) *Family and Parenthood: Supporting families, preventing breakdown.* Rowntree Foundation

Yelloly, M, and Henkel, M (1995) *Learning and Teaching in Social Work: Towards reflective practice.* Jessica Kingsley